James Allen's Book of Meditations

Daily Reflections for Mindful Living

A Modern Translation

Adapted for the Contemporary Reader

James Allen

Table of Contents

Preface - Message to the Reader

Rebuilding the Greatest Library in Human History

Thousands of years ago, the Library of Alexandria was the heart of global knowledge — a sanctuary where the wisdom of every known civilization was gathered and shared freely.

And then, it was lost.

Now, we're rebuilding it — and you are invited to join us.

At the Library of Alexandria, we've set out to make every book available to *every person on Earth* — not just in print, but in every language, every format, and for every reader.

Here's how we do it:

- **Deluxe Print Editions at True Printing Cost** - Order any book as a high-quality paperback, elegant hardcover, or stunning boxset — and only pay what it costs to print. No markups. No middlemen.
- **Unlimited Access to the Greatest Works** - Enjoy thousands of timeless classics — from Plato to Shakespeare to Tolstoy — in beautiful, modern eBook and audiobook editions. Read and listen without limits — for every reader, everywhere.
- **Modern Translations for Every Language & Dialect** - We're reimagining the classics in clear, accessible language — and translating them into every dialect imaginable. Everyone deserves to understand humanity's greatest ideas.

When you visit **LibraryofAlexandria.com**, you're not just accessing books — you're joining a global movement to restore, preserve, and share the wisdom of civilization.

Join us today at LibraryofAlexandria.com

Together, we'll ensure the light of human wisdom never fades again.

With gratitude,
The Modern Library of Alexandria Team

Visit:

www.libraryofalexandria.com

Or scan the code below:

Introduction

The Quiet Companion to a Thoughtful Life:
A Year of Spiritual Renewal with James Allen

James Allen's Book of Meditations for Every Day in the Year stands apart from his other works not just in form, but in spiritual function. Where his foundational texts like As a Man Thinketh, The Mastery of Destiny, and From Passion to Peace are essays in moral and spiritual philosophy, this volume takes a more intimate approach. Composed as a collection of daily reflections—short meditations, poetic lines, and distilled insights—this book serves as a practical tool for spiritual alignment and mindful living. It was crafted to be read one day at a time, allowing Allen's transformative philosophy to gently infuse a reader's life with clarity, peace, discipline, and moral courage.

First published posthumously by his wife Lily Allen in 1913, this collection offers readers a way to live alongside Allen's teachings—not simply to study them intellectually, but to absorb them through daily repetition and personal reflection. Each passage carries the full weight of Allen's moral clarity, spiritual poise, and commitment to inner excellence. These are not casual affirmations or vague spiritual encouragements. They are precise, distilled, and often deeply challenging statements of spiritual law and inner truth. This is James Allen at his most concentrated—a voice of purpose, integrity, and inner stillness, speaking directly to the soul.

This modern edition, Daily Reflections for Mindful Living – A Modern Translation – Adapted for the Contemporary Reader, brings Allen's meditations into clear and present focus. While the original style is poetic and Victorian in tone, this updated version renders the

3

language accessible to the modern reader while preserving Allen's ethical sharpness and spiritual warmth. The goal is to maintain the meditative cadence and daily rhythm of the original while ensuring the words resonate immediately with today's spiritual seekers.

Meditation as Practice:
Cultivating Inner Stillness Through Daily Reflection

Allen believed that true spiritual growth must be practiced daily. Just as the body is sustained by daily nourishment, so must the mind and soul be nurtured by daily contemplation. In this book, he offers a simple yet profound way to do so: one brief meditation each day, each rooted in a fundamental truth about life, thought, and character. These meditations are designed to center the reader, to clarify their intentions, and to help them remember the higher purpose behind all action.

The topics Allen addresses over the course of the year are remarkably varied: self-control, purity, forgiveness, clarity, effort, silence, compassion, right thought, duty, joy, discipline, and divine union. Though each meditation is brief—sometimes no more than a few sentences—its spiritual impact can be enormous when taken seriously. Allen intended these short passages not as intellectual content, but as tools of transformation. Read slowly, intentionally, and repeatedly, they shape the mind and awaken the heart.

Unlike passive inspiration or fleeting motivation, Allen's meditations invite active participation. They ask the reader to look inward—to examine thought patterns, attitudes, and emotional responses. They call for reflection, self-honesty, and, ultimately, self-transcendence. In this way, Allen's work functions not just as a literary collection, but as a yearlong spiritual discipline.

Each meditation can also act as a mirror, reflecting back to the reader the current state of their own inner life. On days of clarity and calm, a passage may feel affirming. On days of confusion or conflict, the same passage may feel like a challenge or correction. This dynamic engagement is part of the book's spiritual genius—it grows with the reader, revealing new dimensions as their inner understanding deepens.

Allen also weaves poetry and rhythm into these reflections, allowing the beauty of language to enhance the truth of the message. While some lines resemble scripture in tone, others feel like soft counsel from a trusted friend. Together, they form a full spectrum of spiritual energy—from stillness to action, from surrender to strength.

Why This Book Matters:
James Allen's Gift of Daily Awakening

In a time when digital noise and hurried distraction dominate modern life, the discipline of daily meditation is more vital than ever. James Allen's Book of Meditations offers an antidote to that chaos. It doesn't ask the reader to withdraw from the world, but to engage with it more consciously—anchored in truth, guided by principle, and illuminated by inner peace.

This work belongs on the bedside table, in a journal, or on the quiet morning desk. It's not a book to be consumed in one sitting, but to be lived with—page by page, day by day. It becomes a daily companion, a teacher that is both gentle and exacting, a reminder that the greatest changes in life begin not in the world, but in the mind and soul.

What makes this book unique is not just its structure, but its integrity. Allen never panders or simplifies. He respects the reader's intelligence and soul, offering deep truths without dilution. And yet, the structure makes those truths digestible, even for those new to spiritual practice. You don't need to understand everything on the first reading—just a willingness to return to the page tomorrow, and the next day, and the next.

This modern adaptation keeps the heart of Allen's message fully intact. The timelessness of his teaching requires no embellishment—only clarity of expression. Each meditation is designed to be a doorway to deeper insight, an invitation to pause, breathe, and return to one's inner center. Over time, these simple daily practices accumulate, creating a quiet revolution within.

Ultimately, James Allen's Book of Meditations is a tool for spiritual alignment. It reminds us that peace is not an accident, joy is not random, and strength is not reserved for a few. These are all the results of right thought, daily effort, and inner cultivation. Allen's meditations gently but firmly point us toward that truth, one day at a time.

May this modern edition become for you what it has been for many over the last century: a daily friend, a moral compass, and a silent voice calling you back to the life of depth, wisdom, and peace.

By Thought we rise; by Thought we fall.
By Thought, we stand or move; all destiny is shaped
By its powerful force. And the one who masters Thought,
Who controls his desires,
And chooses and forms thoughts of Love and Light,
Shapes his highest goal in the flawless Light of Truth.

The one who cannot find
The way of Meditation will never reach
Freedom and enlightenment.
But you will find the way of Holy Thought;
With a mind that is calm and steady, you will see
What is permanent in the midst of change,
The eternal Truth in things that come and go.

You will understand the Perfect Law:

Order rises from chaos when the self is conquered
And lies beneath the control of man. Let Love be your strength.

Look at the crowds suffering from their passions,
And have compassion for them. Understand their pain
By remembering the sorrow you have overcome. You will come
To perfect peace, and through that, you will bless the world,
Leading those who seek to the High and Holy Way.

Now I return to my Abode;

James Allen's Book of Meditations For Every Day in The Year

January First.

Often, the person driven by emotions is the first to try to fix others, but the wise person works on fixing themselves. If someone wants to change the world, they should start by changing themselves. Self-improvement doesn't stop at removing harmful habits—that's just the beginning. It ends when every selfish thought and goal is defeated. Until we reach total purity and wisdom, there will always be some form of personal weakness or ignorance that needs to be overcome.

Through aspirations, we rise from the earth to heaven, from ignorance to knowledge, from darkness to light. Without aspirations, we remain like animals—earthly, driven by desires, and lacking enlightenment. Aspiration is the desire for higher, spiritual things.

Where can peace be found? Where does truth hide?

January Second

First things first—work before play, duty before pleasure, others before yourself. This is a solid rule that will never mislead you. Starting right is half the victory. An athlete who starts poorly may lose the race; a merchant who starts badly may lose his reputation; and a truth-seeker who starts wrong may miss the crown of righteousness. To begin with pure thoughts, strong integrity, selfless goals, noble aims, and an honest conscience is to start right. When we put first things first, everything else falls into place, making life simple, beautiful, successful, and peaceful.

The soul cries out for its lost inheritance.

If someone seeks peace, they must leave behind their passions.

January Third

As long as someone finds pleasure in their base desires, they cannot aspire to something greater. They are satisfied where they are. But when the sweetness turns bitter, they begin to long for higher things. When earthly joys are taken away, they start seeking heavenly joy. It's when impurity leads to suffering that purity is pursued. Truly, aspiration rises like a phoenix from the ashes of repentance, and on its wings, we can reach the highest heavens.

The person with aspiration is on the path to peace, and if they don't give up, they will reach that goal. If they constantly renew their mind with glimpses of the heavenly vision, they will reach a heavenly state.

What can be imagined can be achieved.

Our lives are shaped by our own thoughts and actions.

January Fourth

We succeed as much as we aspire. Our desire to achieve is the measure of what we can become. To focus the mind is to guarantee success. Just as we can experience and understand low things, we can experience and understand high things. Just as we have become human, we can become divine. Turning the mind towards higher and divine thoughts is the most important task.

What is impurity but the impure thoughts of the thinker? What is purity but the pure thoughts of the thinker? No one else does our thinking for us. Each of us is pure or impure by our own choices. The person with aspiration sees the path leading upward to heaven and already feels a taste of the final peace.

There is a life of victory over sin and triumph over evil.

When a person truly wants and decides, they can find what is good and true.

January Fifth

The Gates of Heaven are always open, and no one is kept out except by their own choices. No one can enter Heaven while they are in love with the pleasures of hell or while they give in to sin and sorrow.

There is a larger, higher, nobler, and more divine life than the life of sin and suffering that most people are trapped in. This higher life is full of victory over sin, triumph over evil, wisdom, happiness, kindness, peace, and virtue. It can be found and lived now. The person who lives it stands firm during changes, remains calm among the restless, and stays peaceful even in the midst of conflict.

Every moment is a chance to choose, and every hour shapes our destiny.

The lover of a pure life renews their mind daily.

January Sixth

Just as a hardworking business person is not discouraged by obstacles but figures out how to overcome them, the person of constant aspiration is not defeated by temptations but instead thinks about how to strengthen their mind. Temptation, like a coward, only sneaks in through weak and unguarded areas. The person facing temptation should carefully study its nature and cause because until it's understood, it cannot be defeated. To overcome temptation, we must understand that it arises from our own ignorance and mistakes, and we must work through meditation and self-examination to remove ignorance and replace it with truth.

A person must know themselves if they are to know truth. Self-knowledge leads to self-control.

Spend time daily meditating on Truth and striving to achieve it.

As errors and impurities are revealed, cleanse them from your mind.

January Seventh

Every step upward means leaving something behind. We only reach the heights by giving up what is low. We only get what is good by letting go of evil. We only gain knowledge by getting rid of ignorance. Every achievement has a price, and it must be paid fully. Every creature has some gift or power that humanity, in its upward journey, has let go of in exchange for something greater. How much we lose by holding on to selfish habits! Behind every small sacrifice, there is an opportunity waiting to lift us to greater knowledge and wisdom.

Let those who have reached higher ground guard themselves against falling back. Be careful with small things, and protect yourself against the entrance of sin.

Strive eagerly for a perfect life.

The struggles of the world all stem from one root cause: individual selfishness.

January Eighth

All the different activities of human life are rooted in one place—the human heart. The cause of all suffering and happiness is not in the outer world but within the heart and mind. Every outside force is supported by the energy it draws from human actions.

The person who cannot face their mistakes and shortcomings but tries to hide them is not ready to walk the path of Truth. They are not prepared to fight against and overcome temptation. A person who

11

cannot face their own lower nature cannot climb the tough path of renunciation.

Each person follows the laws of their own being, not the laws of others.

When the soul is most tested, its need is greatest.

January Ninth

Don't lose hope because of failure. Each failure holds a special lesson and wisdom to be gained. No teacher can lead us to greatness more surely than the lessons we learn from failure. Every mistake and every fall carries a valuable lesson if we search for it. Those who look for the good in what seems to be a disaster will rise above every event and use their failures as stepping stones to greater success.

Foolish people blame others for their mistakes and sins, but truth-lovers take full responsibility for their actions. Let them admit their responsibility for their own behavior.

Where temptation is strong, the greater and longer-lasting the victory will be.

The soul's greatest need is for what is permanent.

January Tenth

The old must go before the new can come. The old house must be torn down before the new one can be built. The old mistakes must be destroyed before the new truth can appear. The old self must be given up before the new person can be born. When the old self, full of anger, impatience, jealousy, pride, and impurity, has been removed, the new person, full of kindness, patience, goodwill, humility, and purity, will take its place. Let the old life of sin and sorrow go away and let the new life of righteousness and joy come in. Then everything that was old and ugly will be made new and beautiful.

In this realization lies the Kingdom of Heaven, the soul's eternal home, and the source of every lasting blessing.

A life of virtue is noble and excellent.

What happens on the outside doesn't matter much because it only reflects what's inside.

January Eleventh

The failure of many outer and isolated reforms comes from the fact that those who follow them treat them as ends in themselves, failing to see that they are just steps toward personal perfection.

All true change must come from within, from a changed heart and mind. Giving up certain foods and drinks and breaking away from some outer habits are good and necessary first steps, but they are only beginnings. To stop there is to fall far short of a true spiritual life. It's better to cleanse the heart, correct the mind, and grow in understanding because the most important thing is a renewed heart.

It matters more what you are within, for everything outside will reflect and be shaped by that.

Renew your commitment every day, and when faced with temptation, don't stray from the right path.

January Twelfth

The days are getting longer. Each day, the sun rises a little higher and the light stays a little longer. In the same way, each day, we can strengthen our character; each day, we can open our hearts a little more to the light of Truth and let the Sun of Righteousness shine more brightly in our minds. The sun doesn't grow bigger or brighter, but the earth turns toward it and receives more light. All the truth and good in the world is already here; it doesn't increase or decrease. But as we turn towards it, we receive its light and blessings in greater and greater amounts.

Just as a craftsman becomes skilled by daily practice with their tools, so we gain skill in doing good by daily practice of the Truth.

You can only learn the Truth through practice.

The wise purify their thoughts.

January Thirteenth

Every day is a new beginning, holding new possibilities and new achievements. The stars have moved in their orbits for ages, but no day like today has ever been seen before. It is a new reality, offering new hope and opportunities to all. In this day, you can become a new person. It can be a day of regeneration, renewal, and rebirth. From the mistakes and sorrows of the past, you can rise as a new person, filled with power and purpose, inspired by a new ideal.

Be pure in mind and body. Let go of selfish pleasures. Clear your mind of selfish thoughts and live a life of high purity.

Be upright, gentle, and pure-hearted.

Always work towards reducing evil and increasing good.

January Fourteenth

All victories, no matter the kind, come after preparation. Victory, like a mountain or a flower, doesn't just happen out of nowhere. It's the result of growth, of causes and effects over time. Just wishing for something or saying magic words won't lead to success in the world; it requires a series of well-planned efforts. Spiritual victories don't happen just when temptation comes. All spiritual victories are won in the quiet hours of meditation and through small successes in daily trials. When the moment of great temptation comes, it is just the climax of a conquest that long preparation has already made sure of.

Focus your mind on practicing virtue and understanding noble principles.

The Never-Ending Joy awaits your return home.

January Fifteenth

Just as rain prepares the earth for crops, sorrow prepares the heart for wisdom. The clouds may darken the sky, but they also refresh and nourish the earth. Similarly, grief clouds the heart, but it also prepares it for greater things. The time of sorrow is a time for reverence. It silences shallow jokes, cruel words, and harsh criticism. It softens the heart and deepens the mind. Wisdom is mostly the memory of what sorrow has taught us.

Don't think that your sorrow will last forever; it will pass like a cloud.

When selfishness ends, grief fades away.

Live happily and kindly, as is fitting for true men and women.

January Sixteenth

There is no greater happiness than being occupied with good thoughts, good actions, or good work. Every good thing brings happiness, and evil cannot enter a heart or home filled with goodness. The mind that is guarded by good thoughts keeps unhappiness out, like a well-guarded city keeps out enemies. Even if unhappiness tries to enter, it cannot fully take over unless it finds the person occupied with evil. Not thinking bad thoughts, not doing bad things, not engaging in harmful activities—all these lead to happiness.

True happiness is the soul's natural and rightful state.

Everything follows a pattern and is governed by the law of cause and effect.

January Seventeenth

Don't worry about results or be anxious about the future. Instead, focus on your own shortcomings and work to remove them. Remember this simple truth—right actions do not lead to wrong outcomes, and a good present cannot create a bad future. You are responsible for your actions, but not for the outcomes. The actions of today bring the joy or sorrow of tomorrow. So focus on what you think and do now rather than what may or may not happen later. The person who does good doesn't worry about the results and is free from fear of future troubles.

The Law reigns forever, and Justice and Love are its eternal servants.

Speak only words that are true and sincere.

January Eighteenth

The storm may rage outside, but it cannot touch us if we have peace within. Just as we feel safe by the fireside during a storm, so the heart that holds on to the Truth stays peaceful even when everything around it is in chaos. The harsh criticism of others and the turmoil of the world cannot make us bitter or restless unless we let it. In fact, if we have peace in our hearts, the outer struggles will only deepen our peace and make us even more committed to spreading peace and understanding.

Blessed is the person who has no wrongs to remember, no injuries to forget, and whose pure heart has no room for hateful thoughts about others.

Those who speak ill of others cannot find peace.

Purification is always hard, and all growth comes with pain.

January Nineteenth.

When a storm passes and everything becomes calm again, notice how nature seems to rest in peaceful silence. Everything seems to take part in the quiet recovery, even things that aren't alive. In the same way, when a burst of passion or strong emotion settles down, the mind enters a time of reflection, a moment of peace, where everything becomes clear and things are seen in their true form. It's wise to use these peaceful times to gain a better understanding of ourselves and to judge others more kindly. The moment of calm is the time for healing.

Joy comes and fills the heart that has emptied itself of selfishness. It stays with the peaceful and reigns with those who are pure. Make every thought, word, and action sweet and pure.

In dark times of sorrow, people come closer to Truth.

January Twentieth.

When tears fall and the heart aches, remember the sorrow of the world. When you experience sorrow, remember that everyone does; no one escapes it. Sorrow is a part of life that makes religion necessary. Don't think your pain is unfair or that it happens only to you. It's just a piece of the greater pain of the world. It's something we all go through. Understanding this can help your sorrow lead you to a deeper spirituality, a broader compassion, and a gentler love for all people and creatures. Let it help you grow in love and peace.

Remember, nothing happens to you that doesn't belong to you or isn't meant for your eternal good.

The end of sorrow is joy and peace.

The state without sorrow is reached through sorrow.

January Twenty-first.

Just as light replaces darkness and calm follows a storm, gladness replaces sorrow, and peace comes after pain. The deeper wisdom that comes from understanding sorrow brings a holier and more lasting joy than the shallow excitement that comes before sorrow. Between the smaller joys of the senses and the greater joy of the spirit lies the dark valley of sorrow that all must pass through. But once through it, the heavenly Joy, the lasting Gladness, becomes our companion. Those who have moved from an earthly path to a heavenly one have lifted the veil of sorrow and now see the radiant face of Truth.

The one whose treasure is Truth, who lives according to Wisdom, will find the lasting Joy. Having crossed the sea of illusions, they will reach the Shore without sorrow.

All external oppression is just a shadow of the real oppression within.

January Twenty-second.

In happiness and unhappiness, in joy and sorrow, in success and failure, in victory and defeat, in religion, business, and all circumstances of life, character is the deciding factor. In the mind of every individual lie the hidden causes of everything that affects their outer life. Character is both the cause and the result. It is the doer of actions and the receiver of consequences. Heaven, hell, and purgatory are contained within it. A character that is impure and vicious will experience a life without happiness and beauty, no matter where it is placed. But a pure and virtuous character will reflect a life full of happiness and beauty. As you shape your character, so will your life be shaped.

Letting go of selfishness and passion and establishing yourself in right action is the highest wisdom.

Those who stay on the path of holiness and overcome every challenge will understand Truth.

January Twenty-third.

When major difficulties arise and troubles surround you, see these challenges as a call to deeper thought and stronger action. Nothing will come against you that you cannot overcome, and no problem will present itself that you cannot solve. The greater your challenge, the greater your test of strength, and the more complete and victorious your triumph will be. No matter how complex your confusion, there is always a way out, and finding that way will require you to use all your hidden strength, energy, and creativity. When you have mastered what seems determined to defeat you, you will find new strength.

By knowing the Truth through practice and being one with Truth, you become invincible, for Truth cannot be defeated.

Do not look outside or behind for the light and happiness of Truth—look within.

January Twenty-fourth.

We progress by a series of efforts. We grow stronger—mentally or physically—through repeated striving in a specific direction. Repeated effort leads to power. It's by following this principle that athletes train to achieve great feats of speed or endurance. When the effort is focused on intellectual pursuits, it results in unusual talent or genius; when directed toward spiritual goals, it results in wisdom or transcendent greatness. We should not be upset when circumstances push us to greater effort and more sustained exertion. Events are only "bad" to the mind that perceives them that way. They are good to the one who sees them as valuable lessons.

You will find Truth in the small tasks of your duty, even in the hidden sacrifices of your heart.

There is no happiness anywhere until impatience is given up.

January Twenty-fifth.

Worry, anxiety, and irritability cannot fix the problems they're aimed at. They only add more suffering to the troubles that cause them. Cultivating a calm and steady mind is essential if life is to have any measure of usefulness and happiness. The small annoyances—and even the bigger troubles—would soon disappear if met with a calm and unshaken spirit. Personal goals, desires, plans, and pleasures will face setbacks and obstacles. Learning to meet these challenges with wisdom and calm is how we find lasting happiness within ourselves.

When impatience and irritability are set aside, the happiness of a calm, peaceful mind is realized and enjoyed.

The greatest happiness comes to the one who fills their mind with the purest and noblest thoughts.

January Twenty-sixth.

We become wise when we realize that happiness comes from certain mental habits, rather than from possessions or circumstances. Many people imagine they would be happy if they just had more money, more free time, more talent, better friends, or better surroundings. But such wishes are empty. Happiness is not found in things. If happiness isn't found within, it will never be found outside. The happiness of a wise mind remains through all changes and challenges.

Your entire life is a series of outcomes created by your thoughts—by your own thoughts.

A sweet and happy soul is the ripened fruit of experience and wisdom.

January Twenty-seventh.

Nature has infinite patience, which is worth thinking about. A comet may take a thousand years to complete its orbit. The sea may take ten thousand years to wear away the land. The evolution of humanity may take millions of years. These facts should make us ashamed of our hurry, fussiness, and self-importance over the small concerns of an hour or a day. Patience leads to greatness, usefulness, and deep peace. Without it, life loses much of its power and joy.

"So, with well-ordered effort, build your structure of Success."

The person who fills their minutes with useful pursuits grows old with honor and wisdom, and success stays with them.

No pure thought, no unselfish act, ever fails to bring about its positive result, and every such result brings happiness.

January Twenty-eighth.

If today is cold and gloomy, is that a reason to lose hope? Don't we know that warm, bright days are ahead? The birds are already beginning to sing, and their songs foretell the love and abundance of a new spring and summer that are still hidden but certain to come. No effort is wasted. The spring of your hopes and dreams is close—very close. And the summer of your good deeds will surely arrive.

Self will disappear, and Truth will take its place.
The Changeless One, the Undivided,
Will live within me and cleanse
The White Robe of the Invisible Heart.

Go to your tasks with love in your heart, and you will go with a light heart and joy.

All evil is corrective and temporary, and therefore not permanent.

January Twenty-ninth.

Through deep self-reflection, strive to understand—not just believe—that evil is temporary and self-made. Understand that all your pain, sorrow, and difficulties have come to you through a perfect law. They have come to you because you deserve and need them. By first enduring them, and then understanding them, you will become stronger, wiser, and nobler. Once you truly understand this, you will be able to shape your circumstances, turn all evil into good, and skillfully weave your destiny.

Stop being a disobedient student in the school of life, and start learning, with humility and patience, the lessons set before you for your ultimate perfection.

Meditation focused on divine realities is the heart and soul of prayer.

January Thirtieth.

Tell me what you think about most often and with the greatest focus. Tell me what your soul turns to in your quiet moments, and I will tell you where you are headed—whether toward peace or pain, toward the divine or the base. We tend to become what we constantly think about. So let the object of your meditation be higher, not lower, so that each time you return to it in thought, you will be lifted up. Let it be pure and free from selfishness so that your heart will be purified and drawn closer to Truth, not dragged down into error.

Meditation is the key to all growth in spiritual life and understanding.

If you constantly think of what is pure and unselfish, you will surely become pure and unselfish.

January Thirty-first.

If you are praying daily for wisdom, peace, greater purity, and a fuller understanding of Truth, yet feel far from these things, it means you are praying for one thing while living out something else. If you stop this conflict—if you stop holding on to things that block you from what you pray for—then you will begin to grow in those very realities. You cannot ask for what you don't deserve. If you want God to grant you love and compassion, you must also give those things to others. When you begin to live and think in the spirit of Truth, you will become one with it.

Enter the path of Meditation, and let Truth be the supreme object of your meditation.

Unrest, pain, and sorrow are the shadows of life.

February First.

Is there no escape from pain and sorrow? Is there no way to break free from the bonds of evil? Is lasting happiness and peace just a dream? No! There is a way, and I say this with joy: evil can be destroyed forever. There is a process by which every negative condition can be removed forever, never to return. There is a practice through which unbroken peace and happiness can be experienced. The beginning of this path is understanding the nature of evil. It is not enough to deny or ignore it—it must be understood.

People stay in evil because they are not willing or ready to learn the lesson it came to teach them.

You must look beyond yourself and start examining and understanding yourself.

February Second.

When rightly understood, evil is not an unlimited power or force in the universe. Instead, it is a temporary phase of human experience and can become a teacher for those who are ready to learn. Evil is not something outside of you; it is an experience in your own heart. By patiently examining and correcting your heart, you will discover the root and nature of evil. Once you understand it, evil will naturally disappear.

There is no evil in the universe that isn't caused by ignorance. If we are ready to learn its lesson, it will lead us to higher wisdom and then vanish.

Every soul attracts what belongs to it, and nothing can come to you that isn't meant for you.

What you are inside creates the world around you.

February Third.

Everything you truly know comes from your own experience. Everything you will ever know must pass through the gateway of your own experience and become a part of you. Your thoughts, desires, and goals make up your world. For you, everything in the universe—whether it's beauty, joy, bliss, or ugliness, sorrow, and pain—is contained within yourself. By your thoughts, you shape your life, your world, and your universe. What you hold in the depths of your heart will eventually, by the law of cause and effect, take shape in your outer life.

Each soul is a complex combination of gathered experiences and thoughts. The body is just a vehicle for expressing them.

To those who seek the highest Good, everything serves the wisest purpose.

February Fourth.

The person who clings to selfishness is their own enemy and is surrounded by enemies. The person who lets go of selfishness is their own savior and is surrounded by friends. Before the divine light of a pure heart, all darkness vanishes, and all troubles melt away. The one who has conquered themselves has conquered the universe.

Come out of your pain, troubles, and complaints by coming out of yourself. Let go of the old, worn-out garment of selfishness and put on the new garment of universal Love. Then you will find the heaven within, and it will reflect in your outer life.

All glory and goodness await the coming of obedient feet.

All human accomplishments first began as thoughts and were then made real.

February Fifth.

When your thoughts are aligned with the greater Law, they are constructive and protective. But when misused, they become destructive. To bring all your thoughts into alignment with an unwavering belief in the power of Good is to work with that Good and to bring about the destruction of all evil within yourself. Believe, and you will live. This is the true meaning of salvation: saving yourself from the darkness of evil by entering into the living light of Good.

It is the silent, powerful thoughts that bring everything into reality.

There is nothing that strong faith and a determined purpose cannot achieve.

February Sixth.

There is no problem too great to be overcome by calm and focused thought. No worthy goal is out of reach if we intelligently use the power of our thoughts. Only when you have deeply examined your inner nature and overcome the enemies that hide there will you understand the incredible power of thought. Thought is directly connected to outward things and has the ability to transform your life. Every thought you have is a force sent out, and depending on its nature and strength, it will seek out and affect other receptive minds. It will also return to you, bringing either good or bad.

Think good thoughts, and they will quickly take shape in your life as good circumstances.

Only the person who has mastered themselves is fit to command and lead others.

February Seventh.

If you want to gain the power to overcome, you must cultivate calmness and stillness. You must be able to stand strong on your own. All power is linked to being unshakable. The mountain, the solid rock, and the sturdy oak tree all speak of power because of their firm and unmoving nature. On the other hand, the shifting sand, the bending twig, and the waving reed speak of weakness because they move easily and cannot stand alone. The person who remains calm and unshaken when others are swayed by emotions or passions is the person of true power.

Those who are fearful, emotional, or shallow need the support of others. But those who are calm, fearless, and thoughtful find strength in solitude. In solitude, their power grows even more.

Have a single aim. Find a meaningful and useful goal, and dedicate yourself completely to it.

Self-seeking leads to self-destruction.

February Eighth.

February Eighth

If you want to truly succeed, don't fall into the belief that doing the right thing will lead to everything going wrong. Don't let the idea of competition shake your trust in the power of doing what's right. I don't care what others say about the laws of competition, because I know the Unchangeable Law that will eventually put those ideas to rest, and it's already doing that in the heart and life of a good person. Knowing this law, I can look at dishonesty with peace of mind, because I know that it will be destroyed in the end. Those who stray from the path of righteousness guard themselves against competition, but those who always do the right thing don't need to worry about such defenses.

No matter what happens, always do what you believe is right and trust the Law. Trust in the Divine Power, and you will always be protected.

Perfect Love is Perfect Power.

February Ninth

A wise and loving heart leads without needing authority. Everything and everyone obeys the person who follows the Highest. He thinks, and it's already done! He speaks, and a world listens to his simple words! His thoughts are in harmony with the Unchanging and Unbeatable

Forces, and for him, weakness and doubt no longer exist. Every thought of his has a purpose, and every action is an achievement. He moves with the Great Law, not pushing against it with his small personal will, and he becomes a channel through which Divine Power flows without obstruction, doing good. He has become Power itself.

Perfect Love is Perfect Wisdom.

If you truly seek Truth, you will be willing to put in the effort to achieve it.

February Tenth

At first, meditation must be separated from daydreaming. Meditation is not dreamy or unrealistic; it's a process of intense, searching thought that strips away everything but the plain and simple truth. By meditating in this way, you won't try to build yourself up in your own opinions, but instead, forget yourself and focus only on seeking Truth. This way, you will remove, one by one, the false beliefs you've surrounded yourself with in the past, and you will patiently wait for the Truth to reveal itself once those errors are removed.

Let your highest goal in meditation be Truth.

As a flower opens its petals to receive the morning light, open your soul more and more to the bright light of Truth.

February Eleventh

Spiritual meditation and self-discipline go hand in hand. So, start by meditating on yourself, trying to understand who you are, because your goal will be to remove all your errors so you can understand the Truth. Begin by questioning your motives, thoughts, and actions, comparing them with your ideal self, and trying to look at them calmly and without bias. In doing so, you will gradually gain more of the mental and spiritual balance that is needed, without which people are like helpless straws tossed on the ocean of life.

Soar upward on the wings of your highest aspirations; be fearless and believe in the greatest possibilities.

February Twelfth

The nature of your first impulse will always shape the results that follow. Every beginning also predicts an end, a goal, or an achievement. A gate opens to a path, and the path leads to a destination; similarly, a beginning leads to results, and results lead to a conclusion.

There are good beginnings and bad beginnings, and each is followed by effects of the same kind. By thinking carefully, you can avoid bad beginnings and make good ones, which will allow you to avoid bad outcomes and enjoy good results. One of the simplest beginnings we face every day is the start of each day's life.

The results will always reflect the cause.

February Thirteenth

Everything in the universe is made up of small parts, and the perfection of something big depends on the perfection of its small parts. If even one small part of the universe were imperfect, the whole would be imperfect. Without a grain of dust, there would be no world, and the whole is perfect because each tiny part is perfect. Neglecting the small things leads to confusion in the big things. A snowdrop is as perfect as a star; a dewdrop is as symmetrical as a planet; and a microbe is just as precisely formed as a human. By laying one stone on top of another, making sure each fits perfectly, the temple finally stands in all its architectural beauty.

When the parts are perfect, the whole will be flawless.

February Fourteenth

The great man understands the immense value of moments, words, greetings, meals, clothes, letters, rest, work, brief tasks, and the countless little things that demand his attention—everything in daily life. He sees all things as divinely assigned, needing only thoughtful and calm action on his part to make life blessed and complete. He neglects nothing, doesn't rush, and avoids error and foolishness. He handles every duty as it comes to him and doesn't delay or regret. By giving himself fully to his closest duty, he attains a simplicity and unconscious power that make him great.

The only way to strength and wisdom is by acting with strength and wisdom in the present moment.

February Fifteenth

The foolish person believes that little faults, small indulgences, and minor sins don't matter. He convinces himself that as long as he doesn't commit major immoral acts, he is virtuous, even holy. But in doing so, he loses his virtue and holiness, and the world sees him as he really is. The world does not respect, love, or admire him; it overlooks him, and he is considered insignificant. His influence is destroyed. The efforts of such a person to make the world virtuous, and his calls for others to give up their big vices, are empty and bear no fruit. The disregard he shows for his small faults weakens his entire character, and it reflects the measure of his manhood.

He who takes his smallest faults seriously becomes a saint.

February Sixteenth

Just as a year consists of a certain number of moments in order, a person's character and life consist of a certain number of thoughts and actions in order, and the finished whole will reflect the quality of the parts. Small acts of kindness, generosity, and selflessness form a kind and generous character. The truly honest person is honest in even the smallest details of life. A noble person is noble in every small thing he says and does. You don't live your life all at once; you live it in pieces, and from these pieces, your whole life is made. You can choose to live each part nobly, and if you do, there will be no trace of baseness in the finished whole.

Being thorough is a form of genius.

Truth is beyond words and can only be lived.

February Seventeenth

Truth is the only Reality in the universe. It is perfect justice, eternal love, and harmony. Nothing can be added to it, and nothing can be taken from it. It doesn't depend on anyone, but everyone depends on it. You can't see the beauty of Truth if you are looking at life through the lens of selfishness. If you are vain, you will color everything with your vanities. If you are lustful, your mind will be clouded with desires, and you'll see everything through the flames of passion. If you are proud and stubborn, you will see nothing but the importance of your own opinions. The humble person who loves Truth knows how to tell the difference between opinion and Truth.

The one who has the most love has the most Truth.

February Eighteenth

You can easily tell if you are a child of Truth or if you are serving yourself, by quietly examining your thoughts, heart, and actions. Do you hold on to thoughts of suspicion, jealousy, lust, and pride, or do you fight against them? If you hold on to them, you are tied to selfishness, no matter what religion you claim to follow. But if you fight against them, you are on the path to Truth, even if you don't follow any religion outwardly. Are you self-centered, always trying to get your own way, or are you gentle, mild, and unselfish, willing to give up your desires? If you are selfish, then selfishness is your master. But if you are unselfish, Truth is what you love.

The signs of a Truth-lover are unmistakable.

Temptation awakens desires that have not yet been conquered.

February Nineteenth

Temptation follows a person who is trying to rise higher until he reaches the divine state of consciousness, and beyond that point, temptation cannot follow. Temptation starts when a person begins to aspire to something better. It stirs up both the good and bad within a person, revealing his true self. A person cannot overcome his weaknesses until he fully understands them. Someone who is just following their basic animal instincts isn't really tempted, because temptation comes only when there is a striving for something better. A person who is content with his sensual desires isn't tempted to fall, because he hasn't yet risen above them.

Aspiration can lift a person to great heights.

February Twentieth

The tempted person should understand that he is both the tempter and the tempted. All his enemies are within himself. The flattery that seduces him, the insults that wound him, and the passions that burn him all come from within the region of ignorance and error where he has been living. Understanding this, he can be sure of winning the battle against evil. When he is deeply tempted, he shouldn't despair but rejoice, because his strength is being tested and his weaknesses are being revealed. A person who admits his weakness will soon start working to gain strength.

If a person cannot face his own weaknesses, he cannot reach the higher path of renunciation.

Seek the path of holiness with determination.

February Twenty-First

Giving up selfishness isn't just about giving up outward things. It's about giving up the inner sins and errors. It's not by giving up fancy clothes, riches, or certain foods, or by speaking in a pleasing way that Truth is found. But by giving up the spirit of vanity, the desire for wealth, the craving for self-indulgence, and by letting go of all hatred, conflict, and selfishness, while becoming gentle and pure in heart, is Truth found.

The renunciation of selfishness is the way to Truth.

February Twenty-Second

A person begins to develop power when he controls his impulses and selfish desires and starts to depend on the higher and calmer consciousness within him.

Realizing unchanging principles within yourself is the source and secret of the highest power.

When, after much searching, suffering, and sacrifice, the light of an eternal principle appears in a person's soul, a divine calm comes over him, and unspeakable joy fills his heart.

A person who has realized such a principle no longer wanders but remains steady and self-controlled.

Only the work built on an indestructible principle will last.

February Twenty-Third

There are few people of true power and influence. It's easy for someone to believe in principles like Peace, Brotherhood, and Universal Love when he is enjoying his possessions. But if, when those things are threatened, he starts calling for war, he shows that he truly believes in conflict, selfishness, and hatred instead.

A person who doesn't abandon his principles, even when he faces the loss of everything, including his reputation and life, is a person of power. He is the person whose words endure, and whom future generations will honor, respect, and admire.

There is no way to gain spiritual power except through inner enlightenment and understanding.

February Twenty-Fourth

All pain and sorrow come from a lack of spiritual nourishment, and aspiration is the cry for spiritual food.

A person's essential nature is spiritual and invisible, and its life and strength come from within, not from external things. Outward things are just channels through which a person's energy flows, but for renewal, a person must return to the silence within. The more a person tries to drown out this silence with the noisy pleasures of the senses and the conflicts of the external world, the more he will experience pain and sorrow. Eventually, this becomes unbearable, driving him back to the inner comfort, the quiet solitude within.

Only in solitude can a person truly understand himself.

Inner harmony is spiritual power.

February Twenty-Fifth

Take the principle of Divine Love and meditate on it quietly and diligently, with the goal of fully understanding it. Shine its light on all your habits, actions, speech, relationships with others, and every secret thought and desire. As you keep up this practice, Divine Love will be revealed to you more and more clearly, and your own flaws will become more obvious, pushing you to keep improving. Once you glimpse the greatness of this eternal principle, you won't be content with your weaknesses, selfishness, or imperfections anymore, and you'll pursue this Love until you've removed everything that stands in its way and have brought yourself into complete harmony with it.

Don't stop until the deepest part of your soul is free of every flaw.

In solitude, a person gains the strength needed to face life's difficulties and temptations.

February Twenty-Sixth

Just as the body needs rest to recover its strength, the spirit needs solitude to renew its energy. Solitude is just as important for a person's spiritual well-being as sleep is for their body's health. Pure thought, or meditation, which happens in solitude, is to the spirit what physical activity is to the body. Just as the body weakens when it doesn't get enough rest and sleep, the spirit of a person weakens when it doesn't get enough silence and solitude. A person cannot stay strong, upright, or at peace unless they regularly withdraw from the noisy outer world and connect with the eternal realities within.

Someone who loves Truth and seeks wisdom will spend a lot of time alone.

Human loves are reflections of Divine Love.

February Twenty-Seventh

People often cling to selfishness and the shadows of evil, thinking that Divine Love is something that belongs to a distant God, something they can never reach. It's true that the Love of God is out of reach for the selfish person, but when the heart and mind are emptied of selfishness, the selfless Love of God becomes a real and permanent part of that person.

This inner understanding of holy Love is the same Love of Christ that is often talked about but rarely understood. It's the Love that not only saves the soul from sin but lifts it above the power of temptation.

Divine Love doesn't know sorrow or change.

February Twenty-Eighth

If a person can't find peace within himself, where will he find it? If he's afraid to be alone with his own thoughts, what stability will he find in the company of others? If he can't find joy in his own thoughts, how will he avoid misery when he's with others? A person who hasn't found anything inside himself to stand on will never find a place of lasting rest. The outside world is full of change, decay, and insecurity, but inside is where all certainty and happiness are found. The soul is complete in itself. Where there's a need, there's also an abundance to fill it. Your eternal home is within you.

Be rich within yourself. Be complete in yourself.

Find your center of balance, and you will succeed in standing alone.

February Twenty-ninth.

Until you can stand on your own, seeking guidance neither from spirits nor mortals, gods nor men, but guiding yourself by the light of truth within, you are not truly free. But don't mistake pride for self-reliance.

Standing on the shaky foundation of pride means you have already fallen. No one depends on others more than the proud person. His happiness is completely in the hands of others. But the self-reliant person stands, not on personal pride, but on an unchanging law, principle, or ideal within himself. On this, he balances himself, refusing to be shaken by either his own passions or the opinions of others.

Find the joy that comes from well-earned freedom, the peace that comes from wise self-control, and the happiness that comes from inner strength.

As water flows from a hidden spring, so does a person's life flow from the hidden depths of their heart.

March First

As the heart is, so is the life. The inside is constantly becoming the outside. Nothing stays hidden. What is hidden only stays so for a time; it eventually grows and comes out. Seed, tree, blossom, and fruit – this is the natural order of the world. From a person's heart comes the conditions of their life; their thoughts bloom into actions, and those actions create character and destiny.

Life is always unfolding from within and revealing itself to the light, and thoughts born in the heart eventually show themselves in words, actions, and accomplishments.

The mind dresses itself in the clothes it makes.

March Second

Let a person realize that life, in its entirety, comes from the mind, and behold, the path to happiness opens up. For then, they will discover that they have the power to control their mind and shape it according to their highest ideals. So, they will choose to walk with strength and determination on the path of excellent thoughts and actions. Life will become beautiful and sacred to them, and sooner or later, all evil, confusion, and suffering will vanish. It is impossible for someone who carefully guards the doorway of their heart to miss out on freedom, enlightenment, and peace.

Anyone who seeks to have a calm, wise, and clear mind is engaging in the greatest task that a person can undertake.

March Third

The mind learns through repetition of its experiences. A thought that is hard to hold onto at first becomes, after constant repetition, a natural and habitual condition. Just as a boy learning a trade can't handle his tools properly at first, but after long practice uses them with skill, so a state of mind that seems impossible to reach becomes, through perseverance, a natural part of one's character.

In this power of the mind to create and recreate its habits lies the foundation of a person's freedom, and the open door to perfect liberty through mastery of oneself.

When the heart is pure, everything outside becomes pure.

March Fourth

A person's life is shaped by their mind, and the mind is made up of habits that, with patience and effort, can be changed and controlled. Once a person realizes this, they hold the key to complete freedom.

But freedom from life's problems (which are really problems of the mind) is a slow process that grows from within, not something that can be quickly gained from outside. Day by day, the mind must be trained to think pure thoughts and to adopt right attitudes until it becomes the ideal of one's highest dreams.

The Higher Life is about living higher in thought, word, and action.

March Fifth

All duties should be considered sacred, and performing them faithfully and unselfishly should be one of the guiding principles of life. Any personal or selfish desires must be set aside when doing one's duty. When this is done, duty is no longer a burden but a joy. Duty only feels burdensome to the person who craves selfish gain or enjoyment. If a person feels their duty is tiresome, they should look within and realize it's not the duty itself that is difficult, but their selfish desire to avoid it.

Anyone who neglects duty, whether big or small, neglects virtue. Anyone who rebels against duty rebels against virtue.

The virtuous person focuses their mind on doing their duty perfectly.

March Sixth

What happens to a person reflects who they are. The destiny that seems to chase them, that they can't escape or avoid, is the inevitable result of their wrong actions. The blessings and curses that come to them unasked for are the echoes of their own actions.

Life is made up of causes and effects. Each action is a cause that must be balanced by its effects. A person chooses the cause (this is free will), but they cannot choose or avoid the effect (this is fate). So, free will gives us the power to start causes, while destiny is the result of living with the effects.

Character is destiny.

March Seventh

All unhappiness comes from a wrong state of mind. All sin is ignorance. It is a state of darkness and lack of understanding. A person who thinks or acts wrongly is like a student in school who hasn't learned their lessons yet. They have to learn how to think and act correctly, in line with the Law.

A student isn't happy when they get their lessons wrong, and no one can find happiness while sin remains undefeated. Life is a series of lessons. Some people learn them diligently and become pure, wise, and happy. Others are careless and remain impure, foolish, and unhappy.

Happiness is the result of a mind in harmony.

March Eighth

Selfishness, or passion, doesn't just exist in obvious forms like greed or uncontrolled emotions. It also hides in every thought that focuses on self-importance. It is most deceptive when it makes a person focus on the selfishness of others, accusing them and talking about it. A person who constantly thinks about the selfishness of others won't overcome their own selfishness. We don't conquer selfishness by blaming others, but by purifying ourselves.

The way to move from passion to peace isn't by throwing blame at others but by overcoming one's own selfishness.

The path to self-conquest is always available.

March Ninth

Through aspiration, a person rises from earth to heaven, from ignorance to knowledge, from darkness to light. Without aspiration, they remain like an animal, earthly, sensual, and uninspired.

Aspiration is the longing for higher things – for righteousness, compassion, purity, and love – while desire is the craving for worldly things like selfish possessions, power, and low pleasures. When a person starts to aspire, it means they are dissatisfied with their lower state and are reaching for something better. It's a sign that they are waking up from their animal-like state and becoming aware of greater possibilities.

Aspiration makes all things possible.

March Tenth

When aspiration touches the mind, it immediately purifies it, and its impurities start to fall away. While aspiration holds the mind, no impurity can enter, for the impure and the pure cannot exist together. However, the effort of aspiration is often short-lived. The mind falls back into its old errors and needs to be renewed constantly.

To thirst for righteousness, to hunger for a pure life, and to rise with joy on the wings of aspiration – this is the path to wisdom and peace.

The lover of the pure life renews their mind daily with the power of aspiration.

March Eleventh

Spiritual transformation is a complete reversal of the usual self-centered attitude toward people and things, and this reversal brings new experiences. The desire for certain pleasures is abandoned and not allowed to take root in the mind, but the energy from that desire isn't lost. It is transformed into a higher form of thought and action. Just as energy is never destroyed but only changes form in the physical world, the mental energy used for lower desires is redirected to higher spiritual activity.

The clear heights of spiritual enlightenment await.

March Twelfth

The early stages of spiritual transformation are painful but brief because the pain is soon changed into pure spiritual joy.

As a person walks the path toward the divine life, they pass through the middle ground of transformation, which is the land of sacrifice. Old passions, desires, ambitions, and thoughts are let go of, but only to return in a more beautiful, permanent, and satisfying form. Just as valuable jewels are thrown into the melting pot, only to be remade into something more beautiful, so too are cherished thoughts and habits given up, only to come back later as new powers and joys, like spiritual jewels polished and shining.

The wise person meets passion with peace, hatred with love, and returns good for evil.

March Thirteenth

The present is the result of everything that has happened in the past. The sum of all a person has thought and done is within them.

It is this understanding of the Perfect Law working through everything that allows a good person to love their enemies and rise above hatred, resentment, and complaints. They know that only what belongs to them will come to them, and even if they are surrounded by enemies, those enemies are just instruments of perfect justice. So they don't blame others but calmly accept their responsibilities and pay their moral debts. But they don't just pay their debts – they make sure not to create any new ones. They watch themselves carefully and make their actions perfect.

Character is the result of repeated habits of mind.

March Fourteenth

Nothing happens by chance; wherever there is a shadow, there is also substance. What comes to a person is the result of their own actions. Just as hard work leads to more work and greater success, and laziness leads to less work and declining success, so every condition of life is the effect of actions.

The vast variety of characters we see in people are the results of past actions, stretching back beyond this life into an infinite past. Life is a great school for developing character, and each person reaps the results of their actions.

Life is a school for character development.

March Fifteenth

A person's life and character are shaped by the thoughts they habitually dwell on. Through practice, thoughts tend to repeat themselves more easily, and they shape character by becoming automatic habits. By dwelling daily on pure thoughts, a person creates the habit of pure and enlightened thinking, which leads to pure and well-performed actions. Through constant repetition, a person becomes one with their thoughts and manifests their purity in actions.

The knowledge of divine truth is gained by living in alignment with purity.

March Sixteenth

Blessed is the day when a person realizes that they are both their own undoer and their own savior. Within them is the cause of all their suffering, but also the source of peace, enlightenment, and godliness. Selfish thoughts, impure desires, and actions not based on truth are the seeds of suffering, while selfless thoughts, pure aspirations, and actions aligned with truth are the seeds of blessedness.

A person who denies selfishness finds the holy place where peace resides.

March Seventeenth

A person who controls their tongue is greater than the best debater. Someone who controls their mind is more powerful than the king of many nations, and someone who fully controls themselves is greater than gods and angels. When a person who is enslaved by their own selfishness realizes they must work out their own salvation, they will rise in dignity and declare, "From now on, I will be a master, not a slave."

Until a person realizes this and begins to purify their inner life, they cannot find the way to lasting peace.

A life of peace and happiness comes through self-control and enlightenment.

March Eighteenth

You will benefit greatly by spending at least an hour each day quietly meditating on moral subjects and how they apply to your daily life. This practice will help you develop calm, inner strength, and improve your ability to see clearly and make good decisions.

Don't rush. Do your duty completely, live a disciplined life, and conquer impulses by following moral and spiritual principles instead of emotions. Believe that, in time, your goals will be fully achieved.

Keep growing, and as you become more perfect, you will make fewer mistakes and suffer less.

March Nineteenth

In every heart, there are two kings. One is a usurper and a tyrant, named Self, whose thoughts and deeds are driven by lust, hatred, passion, and conflict. The other is the rightful king, named Truth, whose thoughts and deeds are rooted in purity, love, gentleness, and peace.

Which king do you serve? Have you crowned the rightful king in your heart? If you can say, "I bow to the King of Truth, and in my heart, I have crowned the King of Peace," then all is well with your soul.

Blessed is the person who finds in their heart the King of Righteousness and bows to Him.

March Twentieth

True peace is a peace that nothing can shake, because it is not a momentary calm between storms but an enduring peace born of knowledge. People don't have this peace because they don't understand. They don't understand because they are blinded by their own errors and impurities. As long as they refuse to let go of these, they will remain ignorant of universal truths.

A person who loves their desires cannot love wisdom.

March Twenty-First

Are our sufferings caused entirely by our own ignorance and wrongdoing, or are they partly caused by others and external conditions?

Our sufferings are just and entirely the result of our own ignorance, mistakes, and wrong actions.

If this weren't true, if a person could do wrong and avoid the consequences, leaving an innocent person to suffer instead, then there would be no law of justice. Without such a law, the universe couldn't exist for a single moment.

While it may appear that people suffer because of others, this is only an illusion, one that a deeper understanding dispels.

A person is not the result of outside conditions; outside conditions are the result of the person.

March Twenty-Second

People suffer because they love themselves and not righteousness. Loving themselves, they also love their illusions, and these illusions keep them bound.

There is one freedom that no one can take away except the person themselves – the freedom to love and practice righteousness.

This freedom belongs to both the oppressed and the oppressor, to the slave and the king. The person who embraces this freedom will cast off every chain. The slave will walk away from their oppressor, who will be powerless to stop them. The king will no longer be corrupted by luxury and will truly be a king.

No oppressor can burden a righteous heart.

March Twenty-Third

The wise person knows. They no longer experience anxiety, fear, disappointment, or restlessness. No matter what condition or circumstance they find themselves in, their calmness will remain.

Nothing will cause them grief. When friends leave their physical bodies, the wise person knows they still exist and does not mourn the shell they've left behind.

No one can harm them because they have connected themselves with that which is unaffected by change.

The knowledge that brings peace is the understanding of unchanging principles, achieved through the practice of pure goodness. When a person becomes one with these principles, they become immortal and indestructible.

Peace belongs to the pure.

March Twenty-Fourth

The flesh flatters, but the Spirit corrects.
The flesh blindly indulges, but the Spirit wisely disciplines.
The flesh loves secrecy, but the Spirit is open and clear.
The flesh holds onto grudges, but the Spirit forgives even the worst enemy.
The flesh is loud and rude, but the Spirit is quiet and kind.
The flesh is changeable, but the Spirit is always calm.

The flesh encourages impatience and anger, but the Spirit responds with patience and peace.

The flesh is thoughtless, but the Spirit is thoughtful.

Hatred, pride, harshness, blaming others, revenge, anger, cruelty, and flattery are the works of the flesh.

March Twenty-Fifth

First, a truth is understood, and then it is realized. The understanding may come instantly, but the realization is usually a gradual process.

You must learn to love by seeing yourself as a child, and as you grow in love, the Divine will unfold within you.

You can only learn to love by constantly meditating on love as a divine principle and adjusting your thoughts, words, and actions each day to align with it. Watch yourself closely, and whenever you think, say, or do something that isn't born from pure, unselfish love, promise yourself to guard against it in the future. By doing this, you will grow purer, kinder, and holier each day, and eventually, you will find that love comes naturally, and you will realize the Divine within you.

When love is perfected in the heart, Christ is known.

March Twenty-Sixth

It is good to become aware of your shortcomings because once you see them and feel the need to overcome them, you will eventually rise above them into the clear atmosphere of duty and unselfish love.

You should not dwell on dark thoughts of the future, but if you think about the future at all, think of it as bright.

Above all, do your duty each day, and do it with a cheerful and unselfish heart. Each day will bring its own share of joy and peace, and the future will hold happiness for you.

The best way to overcome your faults is to faithfully perform all your duties without thinking of personal gain, to do everything you can to make others happy, speak kindly to everyone, do kind acts when possible, and never retaliate when others wrong you.

Put your whole heart into the present, living each minute, hour, and day with self-control and purity.

March Twenty-Seventh

The righteous person has nothing to hide. They commit no acts that need secrecy, and they have no thoughts or desires they wouldn't want others to know. As a result, they are fearless and unashamed.

Their steps are firm, their body upright, and their speech is clear and direct. They look everyone in the eye.

How could they fear anyone when they have wronged no one? How could they be ashamed before anyone when they have deceived no one?

Since they no longer do wrong, they can never be wronged. Since they no longer deceive, they can never be deceived.

It is impossible for evil to overcome good, so the righteous person can never be brought down by the unrighteous.

The person whose heart is at peace with all cannot be troubled by weariness or restlessness.

March Twenty-Eighth

There is a kind of outburst called "righteous anger," and it seems righteous, but when viewed from a higher perspective, it is not righteous at all.

There is a certain nobility in feeling anger toward wrong or injustice, and it is far better than being indifferent, but there is a higher form of nobility, where love and gentleness take the place of anger and achieve much more.

A person who seems to have been wronged deserves our pity, but the person who did the wrong deserves even more compassion because they are ignorantly bringing suffering upon themselves. They must eventually reap the consequences of their actions.

When we fully understand divine compassion, anger and all forms of passion lose their hold on us.

March Twenty-Ninth

Goodness is not weak sentiment, but inner virtue, and its direct result is strength and power. Therefore, a good person is not weak, and a weak person is not good.

We should not judge others harshly, but we can judge our own lives and conduct by their results.

It is a fact that someone can "flourish like a green tree" and still be unrighteous, but we should also remember that the green tree will eventually wither or be cut down, just like the fate of the unrighteous.

It is impossible to be truly exalted without living an exalted life.

March Thirtieth

The true teachers of humanity are few. A thousand years may pass without the arrival of such a teacher, but when one does appear, the distinguishing feature is their life. Their behavior is different from others, and their teaching is not drawn from books or other people but from their own life.

The true teacher lives first and then teaches others how to live. The proof of their teaching is their own life.

Out of millions of preachers, only one is ultimately accepted by humanity as the true teacher, and that person is the one who lives the truth.

The supreme goal of all religions is to teach people how to live.

March Thirty-First

Jesus gave the world a set of simple, clear rules that, if followed, would allow everyone to live the perfect life and become children of God. These rules are so straightforward that even a child could understand them without difficulty.

They all relate directly to human behavior and can only be applied by each person in their own life.

Living by these rules lifts a person into the awareness of their divine nature and oneness with God, the Supreme Good.

Everyone, in their deepest hearts, knows that Goodness is divine.

A person has no character, no soul, and no life apart from their thoughts and deeds.

April First.

Each person is responsible for their thoughts, actions, state of mind, and the life they live. No power, event, or circumstance can force someone into doing evil or being unhappy. A person makes their own choices. They think and act by their own will. Not even the wisest or greatest being—not even the Supreme—can make someone good or happy. Each person must choose goodness for themselves, and through that choice, they will find happiness.

This life of victory is not for those who are satisfied with lesser things; it is for those who deeply desire it and are willing to work for it, who seek righteousness as eagerly as a miser seeks gold. This life is always available and offered to everyone, and blessed are those who accept and embrace it; they will enter the world of Truth and find Perfect Peace.

There is a larger, higher, nobler, and more divine life than one of sinning and suffering.

April Second

A person's life is real; their thoughts are real; their actions are real. To focus on understanding what truly exists is the path of wisdom.

Thinking of a person as something beyond mind and thought is not real, and focusing on things that aren't real leads to foolishness.

A person cannot be separated from their mind; their life cannot be separated from their thoughts. Mind, thought, and life are as connected as light, brightness, and color. The facts are enough, and within them lies all the knowledge we need.

To live is to think and act, and to think and act is to change.

April Third

A person's mind is always changing. They are not something "finished" or "complete," but have the ability to grow and improve.

The purification of the heart, the thinking of good thoughts, and the doing of good deeds—these are calls to a higher, nobler way of thinking. They are forces that urge people to choose thoughts that lift them to greater power, goodness, and joy.

Aspiration, meditation, and devotion are the main ways people throughout time have used to reach higher levels of thought, greater peace, and deeper knowledge. As a person thinks in their heart, so they become. They save themselves from their own foolishness and suffering by creating new habits of thought, becoming a new thinker, a new person.

A person's being is shaped by every thought they have. Every experience affects their character.

April Fourth

Only by choosing wise thoughts, and necessarily by doing wise deeds, does one gain wisdom.

Most people, who are unaware of their spiritual nature, are slaves to their thoughts, but the wise person is the master of their thoughts.

The unenlightened follow blindly, while the wise choose thoughtfully. The masses act on impulse, thinking only of immediate pleasure and happiness; the sage commands and controls their impulses, resting on what is eternally right.

Those who act on impulse break the law of righteousness, but the sage, by controlling impulse, obeys it. The wise person stands face to face with the facts of life. They understand the nature of thought and follow the law of their being.

Thought shapes character, conditions, and knowledge.

April Fifth

The law cannot be unfair. It always works the same way. If we break it, we suffer; if we obey it, we are happy.

It is no less kind to suffer the consequences of wrongdoing than it is to enjoy the rewards of doing right. If we could avoid the effects of ignorance and sin, there would be no security, and there would be no place of refuge, for we could also be denied the results of wisdom and goodness. Such a system would be random and cruel, but the law is one of justice and kindness.

The supreme law is based on eternal kindness, perfect in its operation, and limitless in its reach. It is none other than that "Eternal Love, forever full, forever flowing free" that Christians sing about, or the "Boundless Compassion" spoken of in Buddhism.

Every pain we experience brings us closer to understanding Divine Wisdom.

April Sixth

Those who understand the universe don't mourn over how things work.

Buddha always called the moral law of the universe the Good Law, and it can only be understood as good. In it, there is no evil or unkindness. It is not a cold, heartless force crushing the weak and destroying the ignorant, but a soothing love and a protective compassion that shields the vulnerable and prevents the strong from misusing their power.

It destroys evil and protects good. It cares for the smallest seed and wipes away the greatest wrong. To see it is to have the highest vision; to know it is to experience the highest bliss, and those who understand it live in peace and joy forever.

The wise person submits their will and desires to the Divine Order.

April Seventh

Rise above the temptations of sin and enter the Divine Consciousness, the Higher Life.

There comes a time in a person's growth when, as evil decreases and good increases, a new vision, a new awareness, a new person is born. When this happens, the saint becomes a sage. They have moved from human life to the divine life. They are "born again," and a new series of experiences begins. They gain a new power, and a new universe opens up before them. This is the stage of Transcendence; this is the Higher Life. When this stage is reached, the limited self is left behind, and the divine life is realized. Evil is left behind, and Good is everything.

Just as passion defines the self-life, serenity defines the Higher Life.

April Eighth

When Perfect Good is fully known, calm vision is gained.

The transcendent life is not controlled by passions, but by principles. It is not built on temporary desires but on lasting laws. In its clear atmosphere, the orderly flow of all things is revealed, and there is no longer any room for sorrow, anxiety, or regret.

As long as people are driven by self-centered desires, they load themselves with burdens and worry about many things, especially their own small, troubled, pain-filled selves. They are anxious about their fleeting pleasures, their protection, and their eternal safety.

But in the wise and good life, all of this is left behind. Personal concerns are replaced by universal purposes, and all worries about one's own pleasure and fate are swept away like a bad dream.

The Universal Good is seen.

April Ninth

Evil is just an experience, not a true power.

If evil were a true, independent power in the universe, no one could rise above it. But while it is not a real power, it is a real experience, for all experiences are real in their own way. It is a state of ignorance and lack of development, and as such, it fades away before the light of knowledge, just like a child's ignorance disappears as they learn more or like darkness fades away with the rising light.

The painful experiences of evil vanish as the new experiences of good fill the mind.

The transcendent person is one who has gone beyond the control of the self; they have risen above evil.

April Tenth

Nothing that happens to a good person can cause them confusion or sadness because they understand its cause and outcome.

Looking back on the self-centered life they have left behind, the person who is divinely enlightened sees that all the hardships of that life were their teachers, guiding them upward. The more they understood their lessons and lifted themselves above their struggles, the more those struggles disappeared.

Their purpose, to teach the person, was fulfilled, and they left the person victorious. The lower cannot teach the higher; ignorance cannot instruct wisdom; evil cannot enlighten good. A student cannot set lessons for the teacher.

What is transcended cannot reach what is higher. Evil can only teach in its own realm, where it is the master; in the realm of good, it has no place or authority.

The strong traveler on the road of truth does not accept evil; they only follow the good.

April Eleventh

The one who conquers another is brave, but the one who conquers themselves is truly noble.

By conquering oneself, Perfect Peace is achieved. A person cannot understand or approach this peace until they realize that instead of fighting things outside of them, they must fight the evils within.

A person has already started on the path of sainthood when they realize that the enemy is not outside but within; that their uncontrolled thoughts cause confusion and conflict; that their unchecked desires disrupt their peace and the peace of the world.

If a person conquers lust, anger, hatred, pride, selfishness, and greed, they have conquered the world.

The one who conquers others may later be defeated, but the one who conquers themselves will never be overcome.

April Twelfth

Force and conflict act on people's passions and fears, but love and peace reach and change the heart.

The person who is defeated by force may not be defeated in their heart and may even become a greater enemy than before. But the one who is won over by the spirit of peace is changed at heart. The enemy becomes a friend.

The pure-hearted and wise have peace in their hearts. This peace enters their actions and shapes their lives. It is stronger than conflict and wins where force would fail. Its protection shields the righteous. Under its care, those who are harmless are not harmed. It offers shelter from the heat of selfish struggles. It is a refuge for the defeated, a shelter for the lost, and a temple for the pure.

When divine goodness is practiced, life becomes blissful. Bliss is the natural state of the good person.

April Thirteenth

The person who has found divine love has become a new person.

This Love, this Wisdom, this Peace, this calm state of mind and heart, can be found and experienced by anyone who is ready and willing to understand what giving up the self really involves.

There is no outside force in the universe; the strongest chains that bind people are the ones they have created themselves. People are chained to what causes them suffering because they want to be, because they love their chains, because they believe their small, dark prison of self is sweet and beautiful, and they fear that if they leave that prison, they will lose everything that is real and valuable.

"You suffer from yourselves, no one else makes you, no one else holds you, but you live and die by your own will."

To the divinely wise, knowledge and Love are one and inseparable.

April Fourteenth

The world does not understand selfless Love because it is focused on chasing its own pleasures.

Just as a shadow follows a form, and smoke follows fire, so effects follow causes, and suffering and happiness follow the thoughts and actions of people.

There is no effect in the world that doesn't have a hidden or visible cause, and that cause is always based on absolute justice.

People suffer because, in the past—whether recently or long ago—they planted the seeds of evil. People are happy because they planted the seeds of good.

Let a person meditate on this truth, strive to understand it, and they will start to plant only good seeds and will destroy the weeds they have grown in the garden of their heart.

The whole world is moving toward the full realization of this divine Love.

April Fifteenth.

The world is, and will be for many years, kept away from that Golden Age, which is the realization of selfless Love. You, however, can enter it now if you are willing to rise above your selfishness and leave behind prejudice, hatred, and judgment for gentle and forgiving love.

Where hatred, dislike, and judgment exist, selfless Love cannot stay. It only lives in the heart that has given up all condemnation. A person who understands that Love is at the core of all things, and who has realized the all-powerful nature of that Love, has no place in their heart for judgment.

If men and women follow this path, then the Golden Age is near.

Only those with a pure heart can see God.

April Sixteenth.

A person whose heart is centered in supreme Love does not label or categorize people; they do not try to convert others to their views or convince them of their methods. Knowing the Law of Love, they live by it and remain calm and kind to all. The wicked and the virtuous, the foolish and the wise, the educated and the uneducated, the selfish and the selfless, all receive the blessing of their peaceful thoughts.

You can only reach this supreme knowledge, this divine Love, by continuously working on self-discipline and by gaining victory over yourself, one step at a time.

Enter into this New Birth, and the Love that never dies will awaken within you, bringing you peace.

Where there is pure spiritual knowledge, Love is perfected and fully realized.

April Seventeenth.

Train your mind in strong, fair, and gentle thinking; train your heart in purity and compassion; train your speech to be silent when necessary and to be true and clean. By doing this, you will enter the path of holiness and peace and will ultimately experience immortal Love. By living this way, you will convince others without trying to convert them; you will teach without arguing; and without seeking praise, wise people will recognize you. Without striving for approval, you will win over their hearts. For Love conquers all, it is all-powerful, and the thoughts, actions, and words of Love never die.

This is the realization of selfless Love.

Rejoice! For the morning has come: The Truth has awakened us.

April Eighteenth.

We have opened our eyes, and the long night of fear is over. For so long, we have been asleep in the world of material things and sensations; for so long, we struggled in the painful nightmare of evil. But now, we are awake in Spirit and Truth. We have found the Good, and the fight with evil is finished.

We slept without knowing we were asleep. We suffered without knowing we were suffering. We were troubled by our dreams, but no one could wake us, for everyone else was dreaming too. But then, there was a pause in our dream; our sleep was interrupted. Truth spoke to us, and we listened. Suddenly, we opened our eyes and saw.

We slept and did not see; we were asleep and did not know it. But now we are awake, and we see. Yes, we know we are awake because we have seen Holiness, and we no longer love sin.

How beautiful is Truth! How glorious is the world of reality! How beyond words is the joy of Holiness!

Abandon error for Truth, and illusion for Reality.

April Nineteenth.

To sin is to dream, and to love sin is to love darkness. Those who love darkness are trapped in it; they have not yet seen the light. A person who has seen the light no longer chooses to walk in darkness. To see the Truth is to love it, and compared to it, error has no appeal. The dreamer experiences moments of pleasure and moments of pain; at one point, they are confident, and at another, they are afraid. They are unstable and have no safe place to go. When regret and punishment chase them, where can they escape? There is no refuge unless they wake up.

Let the dreamer struggle with their dream; let them work to understand the false nature of all selfish desires. Then, they will open their spiritual eyes to the world of Light and Truth. They will find happiness, sanity, and peace by seeing things as they really are.

Truth is the Light of the universe, the daylight of the mind.

The Knowledge of Truth is a constant comfort.

April Twentieth.

When everything else fails, Truth does not. When the heart is empty and the world offers no shelter, Truth provides a peaceful refuge and a quiet rest. Life's burdens are many, and its path is full of challenges, but Truth is greater than any burden and overcomes all difficulties. Truth lightens our load and brightens our path with the light of joy.

Loved ones leave us, friends fail us, and possessions vanish. So, where is the voice of comfort? Where is the whisper of peace? Truth is the comforter of those without comfort and the friend of those who are alone. Truth does not fade, fail, or disappear. It offers the lasting peace that consoles us.

Stay awake, and listen so you can hear the call of Truth, the voice of the Great Awakener.

Truth takes the sting out of suffering and clears away the clouds of trouble.

Those who cling to their illusions, loving themselves and sin, cannot find the Truth.

April Twenty-first.

Truth brings joy from sorrow and peace from confusion; it points the selfish toward Good and shows sinners the path to Holiness. Its essence is doing what is Right. To the sincere and faithful, it brings comfort; to the obedient, it gives the crown of peace. I take refuge in Truth: Yes, I stay in the Spirit of Good, in the knowledge of Good, and in the practice of Good. Because of this, I feel reassured and comforted. It is as if malice doesn't exist, and hatred has disappeared. Lust is trapped in the deepest darkness and has no place in Truth's shining Light. Pride is broken and scattered, and vanity fades away like a mist. I have set my sights on Perfect Good, and I walk the Blameless Path. Because of this, I am comforted.

I am strengthened and comforted because I have found refuge in Truth.

A pure heart and a blameless life bring joy and peace.

April Twenty-second.

Our good actions stay with us, saving and protecting us. Evil actions are mistakes. Our evil deeds follow us, and they cause us to fall in moments of temptation. The wrongdoer has no protection from sorrow, but the person who does good is shielded from harm. The foolish person says to their evil deed, "Stay hidden, don't be exposed," but their evil is already known, and their sorrow is certain.

If we are caught up in evil, what can protect us? What can keep us from misery and confusion? No person, no wealth, no power, no heaven, or earth can protect us from confusion. From the results of evil, there is no escape, no safe place, and no protection.

If we are in Good, what can bring us to misery and confusion? No person, no poverty, no sickness, no heaven, or earth can bring us to confusion.

There is a clear path and a quiet rest.

Rejoice and don't be sorrowful, all who love Truth! For your sorrows will pass away like the morning mist.

April Twenty-third.

Disciple: Teacher of teachers, guide me.

Master: Ask, and I will answer.

Disciple: I have read a lot, but I am still ignorant; I have studied many doctrines, but I have not gained wisdom. I know the scriptures by heart, but peace is still hidden from me. Show me, Master, the way of knowledge. Reveal to me the path of divine wisdom. Lead me into the way of peace.

Master: The way of knowledge, Disciple, is through searching the heart. The path of wisdom is by practicing righteousness. A life without sin is the way to find peace.

See where Eternal Love is hidden! (The deathless Love that seemed so far away!) It is revealed in the humble heart to the one who lives a sinless life today.

Great is the challenge you have started, the mighty challenge of overcoming yourself. Be faithful, and you will win.

April Twenty-fourth.

Disciple: Lead me, Master, for my darkness is very great! Will the darkness lift, Master? Will struggle end in victory, and will my many sorrows come to an end?

Master: When your heart is pure, the darkness will disappear. When your mind is freed from passion, your struggles will end, and when you let go of self-preservation, there will be no more sorrow. You are now on the path of discipline and purification; all my disciples must walk this way. Before you can enter the white light of knowledge, before you can see the full glory of Truth, all your impurities must be washed away, all your illusions removed, and your mind strengthened with endurance.

Do not lose your faith in Truth; remember that Truth is always supreme, and know that I, the Lord of Truth, am watching over you.

Be faithful, endure, and I will teach you all things.

Blessed is the one who obeys the Truth; they will not remain without comfort.

April Twenty-fifth.

Disciple: What are the greater and lesser powers?

Master: Listen again, Disciple! By faithfully walking the path of discipline and purification, not turning away from its challenges but accepting its hardships, you will gain the three lesser powers of discipleship, and you will also receive the three greater powers. These greater and lesser powers will make you invincible. Self-control, Self-reliance, and Watchfulness are the three lesser powers. Steadfastness, Patience, and Gentleness are the three greater powers.

When your mind is well-controlled and in your care; when you depend on no external help, but only on Truth; and when you are always watchful of your thoughts and actions—then you will come near to the Supreme Light.

Your darkness will be gone forever, and joy and light will follow your steps.

Be diligent in your effort, patient in your endurance, and strong in your resolve.

April Twenty-sixth.

These four things pollute the heart: the craving for pleasure, the attachment to temporary things, the love of self, and the desire for personal continuation. From these four impurities come all sins and sorrows.

Wash your heart clean. Let go of your cravings for pleasure. Free your mind from the desire for possessions. Abandon thoughts of self-importance.

By giving up all cravings, you will find contentment. By freeing your mind from the love of things that fade, you will gain wisdom. By letting go of self-centeredness, you will find peace.

A pure person is free from desire. They do not crave excitement. They place no value on temporary things. They are the same whether in riches or poverty, in success or failure, in victory or defeat, in life or death. Their happiness is steady, and their peace is sure.

Hold fast to love, and let it guide your actions.

Instruct me in the actions that align with the Eternal, so I may be watchful and not fail.

April Twenty-seventh.

The unrighteous person is controlled by their emotions. Their likes and dislikes rule over them. Prejudices and biases blind them. They desire and suffer, crave and grieve, and they know nothing of self-control, so their unrest is great.

The righteous person is master of their moods. They have left behind childish things like likes and dislikes. They have set aside prejudice and bias. Not desiring anything, they do not suffer. Not craving enjoyment, sorrow does not touch them. Perfect in self-control, they live in great peace.

Do not condemn, resent, or seek revenge. Do not argue or take sides. Stay calm in all situations. Be just, and speak the truth. Act with gentleness, compassion, and kindness. Be endlessly patient. Hold fast to love, and let it guide your actions. Have goodwill toward all, without making distinctions. Think equally of all and let no one disturb you.

Be thoughtful and wise, strong, and kindhearted.

Be watchful, that no thought of self slips back in and stains you again.

April Twenty-eighth.

Think of yourself as gone. In everything you do, think of the good of others and the world, not of your own pleasure or reward. You are no longer separate from people; you are one with everyone. No longer struggle against others for yourself, but feel compassion for all.

Do not consider anyone your enemy, for you are the friend of all people. Be at peace with everyone. Pour out your compassion on all living things, and let boundless kindness fill your words and actions.

This is the joyful way of Truth. This is the doing that aligns with the Eternal.

The person who does what is right lives with joy. They act from principles that do not change or fade. They are one with the Eternal and have moved beyond unrest.

The peace of the righteous person is perfect. It is not disturbed by change or impermanence.

Freed from passion, they are calm and do not grieve. They see things as they are and are no longer confused.

Open your eyes to the Eternal Light.

Knowledge is for those who seek. Wisdom crowns those who strive. Peace speaks in sinless silence. All things perish; Truth remains.

April Twenty-ninth.

Increase your strength and self-reliance. Make the ghosts of your mind obey your will. See that you control yourself and let no mood, no passion, no swift desire throw you into disgrace. But if you are knocked down, rise again, and reclaim your dignity. Learn humility and wisdom from your fall.

Always strive to master your mind. Take some good from every situation that confronts you. Make your strength grow richer from the hardships you face and overcome.

Submit to nothing but nobleness. Rejoice like a strong athlete reaching for the prize when your full strength is tested.

Follow where Virtue leads, higher and higher. Listen when Purity speaks, and don't put out its fire.

Look! The person who reaches upward, cleansed from all desires, will see Reality.

Deliverance will come to the one who strives with struggles, sorrows, tears, and pain until they succeed.

April Thirtieth.

Do not be a slave to lusts, cravings, indulgences, disappointments, miseries, griefs, fears, doubts, and regrets. Instead, control yourself with calmness. Master that part of you that has mastered others and has mastered you before. Do not let your passions rule you. Instead, rule over them. Conquer yourself until your passion transforms into peace, and wisdom crowns you. Then, you will achieve and, by achieving, you will know.

Look within yourself. See! In the midst of change is the Unchanging. At the heart of conflict is Perfect Peace. At the root of all the world's restless striving is passion. Whoever follows passion finds pain, but whoever conquers passion finds peace.

I may be ignorant, but I strive to know, and I will not stop striving until I succeed.

Be encouraged! You will reach the heights of the Blessed Vision.

May First.

Eolaus: I know that sorrow comes after passion. I know that grief, emptiness, and heartache follow all earthly joys. That's why I'm sad. Still, Truth must exist, and if it exists, it can be found. Even though I'm sad, I know that I will be happy once I find the Truth.

Prophet: There is no happiness like the joy of Truth. Those with pure hearts live in constant bliss, never knowing sorrow or pain. How can someone see the universe and be sad? To know is to be happy. Those who have reached Perfection rejoice. They are the ones who live, know, and realize the Truth.

The person who finds self-control finds Truth.

Not in any of the three worlds can the soul find lasting satisfaction apart from realizing righteousness.

May Second.

Every soul, whether consciously or unconsciously, craves righteousness, and each soul tries to satisfy that craving in its own way and according to its understanding. The craving is the same, and righteousness is the same, but there are many different paths to it. Those who seek it knowingly are blessed and will soon find the final and permanent satisfaction that only righteousness can give. They have discovered the true path. But those who seek it unconsciously may enjoy temporary pleasures for a while, but they are not blessed. They are carving paths of suffering that they will walk on with pain and regret, and their soul will cry out for its lost treasure—the eternal treasure of the righteous.

Blessed are those who sincerely and wisely seek.

Glorious, radiant, free, detached from the control of selfishness!

May Third.

The journey to the Kingdom can be long and difficult, or it can be short and quick. It could take a minute, or it could take a thousand years. Everything depends on the faith and belief of the seeker. Most people cannot enter because they do not believe; how can they realize righteousness if they do not believe in it or in the possibility of achieving it? It is not necessary to leave the outside world or your duties in it. In fact, righteousness can only be found through unselfish dedication to one's duties. But everyone who believes and aims to achieve will eventually be victorious if they do not give up, lose sight of the Ideal Goodness, or stop pressing forward to Perfection.

The outward life aligns with the inward harmony.

The regulation and purification of behavior.

May Fourth.

The whole journey from the Kingdom of Conflict to the Kingdom of Love can be summed up in one phrase: the regulation and purification of behavior. If this process is pursued consistently, it will lead to perfection. As a person gains mastery over certain forces within themselves, they begin to understand the laws that govern these forces. By observing the constant cause-and-effect happening within themselves until they fully understand it, they will also understand how it works universally among all people.

This process is also about simplifying the mind, sifting out everything except the essential goodness in one's character.

They no longer live for themselves, but for others, and by doing so, they experience the greatest joy and deepest peace.

Apart from the sincere effort to live out the teachings of Jesus, there can be no true life.

May Fifth.

A good person is the flower of humanity, and to grow purer, nobler, and more like God every day by overcoming selfish tendencies is to draw closer to the Divine Heart. "He who would be My disciple, let him deny himself daily," is a command that no one can misunderstand, though they may ignore it. There is no substitute for Goodness anywhere in the universe. Until a person has Goodness, they have nothing truly valuable or lasting. The only way to possess Goodness is to give up everything that opposes it. Every selfish desire must be removed; every impure thought must be let go; every attachment to personal opinions must be sacrificed. Doing this is what it means to follow Christ.

Above all beliefs, creeds, and opinions is a loving and selfless heart.

To live in love always and with everyone is to live the true life, to have Life itself.

May Sixth.

Jesus lived this way, and all people can live this way if they humbly and faithfully follow His teachings. As long as they refuse to do this, clinging to their desires, passions, and opinions, they cannot truly be His disciples; they are disciples of selfishness. "Truly, truly, I say to you, whoever commits sin is a servant of sin," is Jesus' clear declaration. People should stop deceiving themselves into thinking they can hold onto their bad tempers, lusts, harsh words, judgments, personal hatreds, petty arguments, and cherished opinions and still have Christ. Everything that divides one person from another, or separates a person from Goodness, is not of Christ, because Christ is Love.

Sin and Christ cannot exist together, and whoever accepts the Christ-life of pure Goodness stops sinning.

When Christ is argued about, Christ is lost.

May Seventh.

It is just as selfish and sinful to cling to an opinion as it is to cling to an impure desire. Knowing this, a good person completely surrenders to the Spirit of Love and lives in Love towards all, arguing with no one, condemning no one, hating no one, but loving all. They look past others' opinions, beliefs, and sins to see the striving, suffering, and sorrow in their hearts. "He who loves his life will lose it." Eternal life belongs to the one who obediently gives up their small, limiting, sin-loving, conflict-causing personal self. Only by doing this can they enter the large, beautiful, free, and glorious life of abundant Love. This is the Path of Life, and the Narrow Gate is the Gate of Goodness.

The narrow path is the Way of Renunciation, or self-sacrifice.

A person cannot learn anything unless they see themselves as a learner.

71

May Eighth.

How am I treating others?

What am I doing for others?

How am I thinking about others?

Are my thoughts and actions towards others motivated by unselfish love, as I would want theirs to be toward me? Or are they driven by personal dislike, petty revenge, or narrow-minded judgment? When a person, in the quiet of their soul, asks themselves these questions and applies all their thoughts and actions to the spirit of Christ's first commandment, their understanding will become clear. They will see exactly where they have gone wrong, and they will know what needs to be done to fix their heart and behavior, and how to do it.

Evil is not worth resisting. The practice of good is the greatest excellence.

Personal dislikes, no matter how natural they seem to the selfish person, have no place in the divine life.

May Ninth.

While a person is busy resisting evil, they are not only failing to practice good, but they are also caught up in the same passion and prejudice they condemn in others. As a result of this mindset, they themselves are seen as evil and resisted by others. If a person resists someone, a group, a religion, or a government as evil, they will also be resisted as evil.

If someone thinks it's a terrible wrong to be persecuted and judged, they should stop persecuting and judging others. Let them turn away from everything they once saw as evil and start looking for the good. This principle is so deep and far-reaching that practicing it will take a person far along the path of spiritual knowledge and achievement.

Anyone who keeps the teachings of Jesus will conquer themselves and become divinely enlightened.

Humanity is essentially divine.

May Tenth.

For so long, people have lived in sinful ways that they now see themselves as naturally sinful, cut off from the Divine Source, which they believe to be outside and distant. But humans are, at their core, spiritual beings, made from the same nature and substance as the Eternal Spirit, the Unchanging Reality that people call God. Goodness, not sin, is a person's natural state. Perfection, not imperfection, is their true inheritance. Anyone can experience and realize this right now if they meet the condition, which is the denial or letting go of self—of their intense desires, pride, egotism, and self-centeredness—what St. Paul calls the "natural man."

Jesus, in His divine goodness, understood the human heart, and He knew it was good.

Anyone who wants to see how good people are at heart should throw away all their ideas and suspicions about the "evil" in others and focus on practicing the good within themselves.

May Eleventh.

People have within them the divine power to rise to the highest spiritual achievements. They can shake off sin, shame, and sorrow and do the will of the Father, the Supreme Good. They can conquer all the forces of darkness within themselves and stand free and shining. They can overcome the world and reach the highest peaks of God's glory. People can do all of this by choice, by resolution, and by using their divine strength. But they can only accomplish this through obedience. They must choose meekness and humility. They must give up conflict for peace, passion for purity, hatred for love, and self-centeredness for self-sacrifice. They must overcome evil with good.

This is the holy path of Truth. This is the safe and lasting salvation. This is the yoke and burden of Christ.

The Gospel of Jesus is a Gospel of living and doing.

May Twelfth.

That Jesus was meek, humble, loving, compassionate, and pure is beautiful, but it is not enough. You, too, must be meek, humble, loving, compassionate, and pure. Knowing that Jesus submitted His will to the Father's will is inspiring, but it is not enough; you must also submit your will to the overruling Good. The grace, beauty, and goodness that were in Jesus cannot help you, cannot be understood by you, unless they are also in you. They will never be in you until you practice them. Without living these qualities, Goodness does not exist for you.

Pure Goodness is true religion, and outside of it, there is no religion.

Those who do the Father's will are the ones who shape their actions according to Divine principles.

May Thirteenth.

For us and for everyone, there is no sufficiency, no blessedness, no peace to be found in the goodness of another, not even the goodness of God. Until that goodness is practiced by us, until it becomes part of our being through constant effort, we cannot know or possess its peace and joy. So, you who adore Jesus for His divine qualities, practice those qualities yourself, and you too will be divine.

The teachings of Jesus bring people back to the simple truth that righteousness, or doing what is right, is entirely a matter of personal behavior. It is not some mystical thing apart from a person's thoughts and actions. Each person must be righteous for themselves; each person must be a doer of the word. It is a person's own actions that bring them peace and happiness, not the actions of someone else.

Only those who forgive experience the sweetness of forgiveness.

Christ is the Spirit of Love.

May Fourteenth.

When Jesus said, "Without Me, you can do nothing," He wasn't talking about His physical body, but about the Universal Spirit of Love, which His actions perfectly expressed. His statement is a simple truth: the works people do for selfish reasons are pointless and worthless. As long as a person lives for their own personal gratification, they remain a mortal being, trapped in darkness and afraid of death.

The animal side of a person can never connect with or understand the divine; only the divine can respond to the divine.

Hatred in a person can never align with the Spirit of Love; only Love can understand Love and unite with it.

People are divine. They are made of Love. They can realize this if they let go of the impure, personal elements they have been blindly following and turn to the impersonal Realities of the Christ Spirit.

In this Principle of Love, all knowledge, intelligence, and wisdom are contained.

Love is not complete until it is lived by people.

May Fifteenth.

Every teaching of Jesus requires the complete sacrifice of some selfish, personal desire before it can be followed. A person cannot understand the Truth while holding onto things that aren't real, and they cannot do the work of Truth while clinging to error. As long as someone holds onto lust, hatred, pride, vanity, self-indulgence, or greed, they can't accomplish anything because the works of all these sins are temporary and false. Only when a person turns to the Spirit of Love within and becomes patient, gentle, pure, compassionate, and forgiving, do they begin to do the works of Righteousness and bear the fruits of Life. The vine is not a vine without its branches, and even then, it is not complete until those branches bear fruit.

By practicing love daily in thoughts, words, and deeds, and by keeping out harmful or impure thoughts, a person discovers the eternal Principles of their being.

A person's only refuge from sin is sinless Love.

Before anyone can know Love as the lasting Reality within, they must completely give up all the human tendencies that stop its perfect expression.

May Sixteenth.

A person can only connect themselves to the Vine of Love by giving up all conflict, hatred, judgment, impurity, pride, and selfishness, and by thinking and doing acts of love. By doing this, they awaken the divine nature within that they've been denying and neglecting. Every time a person gives in to anger, impatience, greed, pride, or vanity, they deny Christ and cut themselves off from Love. This is the only way Christ is denied—not by refusing to accept a specific religious belief. Christ is only known to those who, through constant effort, have transformed themselves from sinful to pure beings. Through noble effort, they've let go of their selfishness, which is the cause of all suffering and unrest, and have become wise, gentle, peaceful, loving, and pure.

This glorious realization is the crown of evolution, the ultimate goal of life.

Just as selfishness is the root of all conflict and suffering, Love is the root of all peace and happiness.

May Seventeenth.

Those who rest in the Kingdom don't look for happiness in material possessions. They understand that all these things (money, clothes, food, etc.) are temporary effects that come when needed and leave when their purpose is served. They don't think about them except as side effects of the true Life. Because of this, they are free from worry and anxiety. Resting in Love, they embody Happiness. Standing on the eternal Principles of Purity, Compassion, Wisdom, and Love, they are immortal and know they are immortal. They are one with God, the Supreme Good, and know they are one with God. Seeing the true nature of things, they have no room in their hearts for judgment.

All people are essentially divine, even if they aren't aware of it.

All so-called evil is rooted in ignorance.

May Eighteenth.

Do not think that the children of the Kingdom live in ease and laziness—these are the first sins that must be eliminated when someone begins the search for the Kingdom. They live in peaceful activity. In fact, they are the only ones truly alive, because the selfish life, filled with worry, grief, and fear, is not real life. They perform all their duties with careful attention, without thinking of themselves. They use all their abilities, which are greatly increased, to build up the Kingdom of Righteousness in the hearts of others and in the world around them. This is their work—first by example, then by teaching. They no longer feel sorrow but live in constant happiness, for even though they see suffering in the world, they also see the final Bliss and the Eternal Refuge.

Anyone who is ready can enter now.

Heaven is not some far-off place after death but a real, ever-present Heaven in the heart.

May Nineteenth.

The only salvation that Jesus recognized and taught is salvation from sin and its effects, here and now. This salvation must be achieved by completely giving up sin. Once this is done, the Kingdom of God is realized in the heart as a state of perfect knowledge, perfect happiness, and perfect peace.

"Unless a person is born again, they cannot see the Kingdom of God." A person must become a new creation, and how can they become new if they don't completely give up the old? A person's last state is worse than the first if they think they can still hold onto their bad temper, stubbornness, vanity, and selfishness, while somehow becoming a new creation just by accepting a particular belief or religious rule.

Heaven is where Love rules, and peace is never absent.

To those who are faithful, humble, and true, the glorious Vision of the Perfect One will be revealed.

May Twentieth.

The message of Jesus is truly good news because it reveals to people their divine potential. It tells humanity, "Take up your bed and walk." It shows people that they no longer need to remain in darkness, ignorance, and sin if they believe in Goodness and are willing to watch, strive, and overcome until they have made that sinless Goodness a reality in their lives. In believing and overcoming, people have not only the guidance of Jesus' perfect teachings, but also the inner guide—the Spirit of Truth in their own hearts, "the Light that enlightens every person who comes into the world." As they follow this Light, it will confirm the divine origin of those teachings.

Realize the perfect Goodness of the Eternal Christ.

The Kingdom of Heaven is perfect trust, perfect knowledge, and perfect peace.

May Twenty-first.

The children of the Kingdom are known by how they live. They show the fruits of the Spirit—"love, joy, peace, patience, kindness, goodness, faithfulness, gentleness, self-control"—under all circumstances and challenges. They are completely free from anger, fear, suspicion, jealousy, moodiness, anxiety, and grief. Living in the Righteousness of God, they demonstrate qualities that are the exact opposite of what the world values and often considers foolish. They don't demand their rights, they don't defend themselves, they don't retaliate. They do good even to those who try to hurt them. They show the same gentle spirit toward those who oppose them as they do toward those who agree with them. They don't judge others or condemn any person or system. They live in peace with everyone.

That Kingdom is in the heart of every man and woman.

Find the Kingdom through daily effort and patient work.

May Twenty-second.

The Temple of Righteousness is built, and its four walls are Purity, Wisdom, Compassion, and Love. Its roof is Peace, its floor is Steadfastness, its door is Selfless Duty, its atmosphere is Inspiration, and its music is the Joy of the perfect. It cannot be shaken. Being eternal and indestructible, there is no more need to worry about the future. Once the Kingdom of Heaven is established in the heart, the pursuit of material necessities is no longer a concern. Having found the Highest, all these things are added as the natural result. The struggle for survival ends, and spiritual, mental, and material needs are met daily from the Universal Abundance.

Pay the price—give up yourself completely.

All things are possible now, and only now.

May Twenty-third.

Now is the reality in which all time exists. It is greater than time, an ever-present reality. It knows neither past nor future and is eternally powerful and real. Every minute, every day, every year becomes a memory as soon as it passes and exists only as a faded picture in the mind, if it is remembered at all.

The past and the future are dreams; now is reality. All things happen now; all power, all possibilities, all actions are now. If you don't act and accomplish now, you won't act or accomplish at all. Living in thoughts of what you could have done, or dreams of what you plan to do, is foolishness. Let go of regret, stop anticipating, and act and work now. This is wisdom.

People have all power now.

Stop walking down every side path that leads your soul into the shadows.

May Twenty-fourth.

People have all power now. But not realizing this, they say, "I'll be perfect next year, or in so many years, or in so many lifetimes." Those who live in the Kingdom of God, who live only in the now, say, "I am perfect now," and by avoiding all sin now, and constantly guarding the doorways of their mind, not thinking about the past or the future, and not being distracted, they remain eternally holy and blessed.

"Now is the accepted time, now is the day of salvation." Say to yourself, "I will live my Ideal now; I will be my Ideal now; and I will not listen to anything that tempts me away from my Ideal. I will only listen to the voice of my Ideal." By making this resolution and following it, you will not stray from the Highest and will always live in the Truth.

Show your natural and divine strength now.

Be determined. Have one clear purpose. Renew your resolution every day.

May Twenty-fifth.

In times of temptation, don't leave the right path. Stay calm. When your passions are stirred, restrain and control them. When your mind starts to wander, bring it back to focus on higher things. Don't think, "I can get Truth from a teacher or from books." You can only get Truth through practice. Teachers and books can give instructions, but you have to apply them. Only those who faithfully practice the rules and lessons and rely entirely on their own efforts will become enlightened. The Truth must be earned. Don't be misled by appearances or seek communication with spirits or the dead. Instead, reach virtue, wisdom, and knowledge of the Supreme Law through the practice of Truth.

Trust the Teacher; trust the Law; trust the path of Righteousness.

Put away all doubts and hesitation, and practice the lessons of wisdom with complete faith.

Avoid exaggeration. The Truth is enough.

May Twenty-sixth.

Speak only words that are truthful and sincere. Don't deceive through words, expressions, or gestures. Avoid gossip like a deadly snake, or it will trap you. Anyone who speaks evil of another cannot find peace. Stop wasting time with idle talk. Don't discuss the private lives of others, talk about society, or criticize famous people. Don't accuse others of wrongdoing but meet all offenses with good behavior. Don't judge those who aren't walking the righteous path, but protect them with compassion by walking the path yourself. Quench the fire of anger with the pure water of Truth. Be modest in your speech and avoid rude, silly, or inappropriate jokes. Seriousness and reverence are signs of purity and wisdom.

Don't argue about Truth—live it.

Abstinence, moderation, and self-control are good.

May Twenty-seventh.

Do your duties with complete faithfulness, putting aside all thoughts of reward. Don't let thoughts of pleasure or self-interest distract you from your responsibilities. Don't interfere with others' duties. Be honest in all things. Even under the hardest trials, even if your happiness or life seems at risk, don't stray from what's right. The person with unshakable integrity cannot be defeated, cannot be confused, and escapes the pain of doubt and uncertainty. If someone abuses, accuses, or speaks badly of you, stay silent and self-controlled. Try to understand that the wrongdoer cannot harm you unless you retaliate and let yourself be drawn into the same wrong mindset. Also, try to meet the wrongdoer with compassion, realizing that they are harming themselves.

Those with pure minds never think, "I've been hurt by someone else." They know the only enemy is themselves.

Let your kindness grow until it swallows up your self-interest.

May Twenty-eighth.

Hold no grudges. Control your anger and overcome hatred. Think of everyone and act toward everyone with the same unchanging kindness and compassion. Even in the hardest trials, don't give in to bitterness or speak words of resentment. Meet anger with calm, mockery with patience, and hatred with love. Don't take sides—be a peacemaker. Don't add to division or promote conflict by siding with one person or group against another. Show equal justice, equal love, and equal goodwill to everyone. Don't criticize other teachers, religions, or schools of thought. Don't create barriers between rich and poor, employer and employee, ruler and citizen, or master and servant. Be fair and balanced with everyone, understanding their different duties. By constantly controlling your mind, overcoming bitterness and resentment, and working toward a steady kindness, the spirit of goodwill will eventually be born in you.

Be strong, energetic, and steadfast.

Be fair-minded, wise, and clear-thinking.

May Twenty-ninth.

Apply reason to everything. Test everything. Be eager to learn and understand. Be logical in your thinking. Be consistent in your words and actions. Use the light of knowledge to examine your mind and clear away its errors. Ask yourself tough questions. Let go of assumptions, rumors, and guesses, and hold onto real knowledge. The person who stands on knowledge gained from practice is filled with a humble yet confident strength and can speak the Truth with power. Master the skill of discernment. Learn to tell the difference between good and evil. Understand the facts of life and see how they connect. Wake up your mind to see the order of cause and effect in everything, both mental and physical. When you do this, you'll see how worthless pleasure-seeking and sin are and how glorious and joyful a life of pure virtue is.

Truth exists. There is no disorder.

Train your mind to grasp the Great Law of Cause and Effect, which is perfect justice.

May Thirtieth.

When this happens, you'll see not with physical eyes, but with the pure, focused eye of Truth. You'll understand your nature and see how, as a thinking being, you've evolved through countless experiences. You'll see how you've risen from lower stages to higher ones and how your changing thoughts and actions have shaped who you are. By understanding yourself, you'll understand the nature of all beings and will live in compassion. You'll understand the Great Law not only in general terms but also in how it applies to individuals. Then, self will disappear like a cloud, and Truth will be everything.

Find no room for hatred, no room for self, no room for sorrow.

Be self-reliant, but let your self-reliance be holy, not selfish.

May Thirty-first.

Foolishness and wisdom, weakness and strength, exist inside a person, not in any external thing. They don't come from any outside cause. A person cannot be strong for someone else; they can only be strong for themselves. They cannot overcome for another; they can only overcome for themselves. You can learn from others, but you must achieve for yourself. Put away all external supports and rely on the

Truth within you. A belief will not hold you up in the hour of temptation. You must possess the inner Knowledge that defeats temptation. A speculative philosophy will prove to be nothing when calamity strikes. You must have the inner Wisdom that ends grief. The Unfailing Wisdom is found only through constant practice in pure thinking and good actions, by aligning your mind and heart with what is beautiful, lovable, and true.

Goodness is the goal of all religions.

The motivation for selfless work doesn't come from any theory about the universe, but from the spirit of love and compassion.

June First.

The spirit of love doesn't decrease when a person realizes that perfect justice exists in the spiritual order of the world. In fact, it grows stronger because they understand that people suffer because they don't know any better, because they make mistakes in ignorance. Even those who are "well-off" can suffer more than the poor, as they, too, are reaping their own mixed harvest of happiness and suffering. The teaching of Absolute Justice is not more encouraging for the rich than for the poor. It tells the rich, who are selfish and misuse their wealth, that they will face the consequences of their actions. It also tells those who suffer and are oppressed that they are now facing the results of their past actions. But by sowing good seeds of purity, love, and peace, they will soon reap a harvest of good and rise above their current struggles.

The painful results of all selfishness must be faced and worked through.

A person creates their own happiness and misery.

June Second.

Your fixed mindset shapes your behavior, and from your behavior come the results that bring either happiness or unhappiness. Since this is true, to change the results you must first change your thoughts. To exchange misery for happiness, you need to reverse the mindset and habits that cause misery. Then the opposite result will appear in your mind and life. A person cannot be happy while thinking and acting selfishly, and they cannot be unhappy while thinking and acting unselfishly. Where the cause exists, the effect will follow. A person cannot escape the results, but they can change the cause. They can purify their nature and reshape their character. There is great power in mastering yourself; there is great joy in transforming yourself.

Each person is limited by their own thoughts.

People live in higher or lower worlds depending on the nature of their thoughts.

June Third.

Think of a person whose mind is full of suspicion, greed, and envy. How small, mean, and sad everything seems to them. Lacking any greatness themselves, they see no greatness anywhere. Being low-minded, they cannot recognize nobility in anyone. Since they are selfish, they see only selfish motives behind even the most selfless acts.

Now think of a person whose mind is free from suspicion, who is generous and big-hearted. How wonderful and beautiful their world seems. They see others as trustworthy, and to them, people are trustworthy. In their presence, even the lowest person forgets their usual behavior and, for a moment, becomes like them, catching a glimpse, though briefly, of a higher way of living, a nobler and happier life.

Avoid harboring dark, hateful thoughts and hold onto thoughts that are bright and beautiful.

The small-minded and the big-hearted live in completely different worlds, even if they are neighbors.

June Fourth.

The kingdom of heaven is not taken by force. Instead, the one who lives by its principles receives its key. The violent person moves among violent people, while the saint belongs to a special group that communicates through divine harmony. People are mirrors reflecting what they hold inside. When a person looks at the world, they are looking into a mirror that shows them their own reflection.

Each person lives within the limits of their own thoughts, and anything outside those limits is invisible to them. They only know what they have become. The smaller their mind, the more certain they are that there is nothing more beyond it. A small mind cannot comprehend a greater one, and understanding the larger mind only comes through personal growth.

People, like students, find themselves in a grade or level that their ignorance or knowledge allows them to be in.

The material world is the other half of the world of thoughts.

June Fifth.

The inner world shapes the outer world. The greater includes the smaller. The physical world reflects the mind. Events are streams of thought, and circumstances are the results of thoughts. The actions and situations that people are involved in are deeply connected to their own mental development. A person is part of their surroundings, not separate from others, and is tied to them through their actions and the fundamental laws of thought that form human society.

You cannot change external things to suit your temporary desires, but you can set aside your desires and change your attitude toward those things. When you do that, the things themselves will appear different. You cannot control the actions of others toward you, but you can control how you act toward them.

Things follow thoughts. Change your thoughts, and your world will change, too.

The highest duty and greatest achievement of a person is perfecting their actions.

June Sixth.

The cause of your suffering or freedom lies within you. Any harm that comes to you from others is the result of your own actions and attitude. They are just the instruments; you are the cause. Destiny is the ripened fruit of your own actions. Everyone receives the fruit of life—both the sweet and the bitter—in fair measure.

The righteous person is free. No one can hurt them, no one can destroy them, and no one can take away their peace. Their understanding of people disarms others' power to harm them. Any injury others attempt to inflict on them bounces back and harms the offender, leaving the righteous person untouched. The good that flows from them is their constant source of happiness and strength. Its root is calmness, and its blossom is joy.

External things and actions cannot harm you.

The person is the most important factor.

June Seventh.

A person often imagines they could do great things if they weren't held back by circumstances—by a lack of money, time, influence, or freedom from family responsibilities. But in reality, these things aren't holding them back at all. The person mistakenly gives them power they don't have and submits, not to these things, but to their own weak thoughts about them. The real thing that holds them back is their own mindset. When they start to see their circumstances as challenges that spur their inner strength, when they realize that their supposed obstacles are actually the steps that will lead them to success, then their problems become opportunities.

The person who complains about their circumstances has not yet become a true person.

Nothing can stop us from achieving the goals of our life.

June Eighth.

A person's power lies in their ability to choose and decide. People do not create the universal laws or conditions—they exist naturally and cannot be created or destroyed. People discover these laws, they don't make them. Ignorance of these laws is the root cause of suffering in the world. To defy these laws is foolishness and leads to bondage.

Who is freer, the thief who breaks the laws of his country or the honest citizen who obeys them? Who is freer, the fool who thinks he can live however he wants, or the wise person who chooses to do only what is right?

People are creatures of habit, and that cannot be changed. But they can change their habits. They cannot change the law of their nature, but they can adapt their nature to that law.

A good person is someone whose thoughts and actions are good habits.

They master the lower part of themselves by serving the higher.

June Ninth.

People repeat the same thoughts, actions, and experiences over and over again until they become part of their character. Growth is the accumulation of thoughts and actions. The person you are today is the result of millions of repeated thoughts and actions. You are not born ready-made—you become, and you are still becoming. Your character is shaped by your choices. The thoughts and actions you choose become habits, and through habit, they become who you are.

Each person is an accumulation of their thoughts and actions. The qualities that seem to come naturally are actually lines of thought and action that have been repeated for so long that they've become automatic. This is the nature of habit: it eventually becomes unconscious and continues without any apparent effort or choice from the person. Over time, it takes such control over the person that it seems as though their will cannot oppose it.

Habit is repetition. Ability is fixed habit.

People are bound by their thoughts.

June Tenth.

It's true that people are influenced by mental forces—in fact, they are those forces. But these forces are not blind, and a person can direct them into new channels. In other words, a person can take control of themselves and change their habits. Although it's also true that a person is born with a certain character, that character is the product of countless lives in which it was slowly built up through choices and efforts. In this life, it will be shaped further by new experiences.

No matter how helpless a person may feel under the control of a bad habit or negative trait—and these are essentially the same thing—they can break free from it and change, as long as they remain sane.

A changed mindset changes character, habits, and life.

The body reflects the mind.

June Eleventh.

A person who suffers from physical illness won't necessarily be healed immediately when they start to shape their mind according to moral and harmonious principles. In fact, for a time, while the body is adjusting and recovering from the effects of past imbalances, the condition may even seem to worsen. Just as a person doesn't gain perfect peace immediately when they start living righteously—except in rare cases—they usually have to go through a painful adjustment period. The same is true with health: it takes time for both the body and mind to readjust. Even if perfect health isn't achieved, it will be improved. If the mind becomes strong and balanced, the body's condition becomes secondary and will no longer be as important as many people make it.

Mental harmony, or moral wholeness, leads to physical health.

Reach out for a deeper understanding of the Infinite.

June Twelfth.

While people try to convince themselves that earthly pleasures are real and satisfying, pain and sorrow constantly remind them of their false and temporary nature. People are always trying to believe that they can find complete satisfaction in material things, but deep down, they feel an inner rebellion against this belief. This rebellion is proof that humans are more than just mortal beings; it shows that true and lasting satisfaction can only be found in the immortal, the eternal, and the infinite.

People are spiritually divine and eternal. Even though they are surrounded by mortality and unrest, they are striving to become aware of their true nature.

The common foundation of faith, the root and source of all religion, is the heart of Love.

The peaceful Reality of the Eternal Heart.

June Thirteenth.

The spirit of a person is inseparable from the Infinite, and nothing short of the Infinite can satisfy them. The burden of pain will continue to weigh on their heart, and the shadows of sorrow will continue to darken their path until they stop wandering in the dream world of material things and return to their home in the reality of the Eternal.

Just as the smallest drop of water contains all the qualities of the ocean, so a person, though separated in their awareness from the Infinite, carries the likeness of the Infinite within themselves. And just as a drop of water must, by the law of nature, eventually return to the ocean, so must a person, by the law of their nature, eventually return to their source and merge with the Infinite.

Becoming one with the Infinite is the ultimate goal of humanity.

Enter into perfect harmony with the Eternal Law, which is Wisdom, Love, and Peace.

June Fourteenth.

This divine state can never be fully understood by a person who is focused on themselves. Personality, separateness, and selfishness are all the same and are the opposite of wisdom and divinity. When a person completely lets go of their selfishness, separateness, and personal desires, they enter into their divine inheritance of immortality and infinity.

The worldly and selfish mind sees this surrender as the greatest loss, but in reality, it is the greatest blessing, the only real and lasting gain. The mind that does not understand the inner laws of life and the nature of its own existence clings to temporary appearances—things that have no lasting value. By holding onto these illusions, it perishes, at least temporarily, in the ruins of its own false beliefs.

Love is universal, supreme, and all-sufficient. This is the realization of selfless love.

When a person's soul is clouded with selfishness in any form, they lose the ability to clearly see spiritual truths and confuse the temporary with the eternal.

June Fifteenth.

People hold onto and indulge the flesh as if it will last forever, and even though they try to ignore how close death is and how certain it is, the fear of losing everything they cling to haunts their happiest moments. The shadow of their own selfishness follows them like an unstoppable force.

As they gather more comforts and luxuries, their inner divine nature becomes numb, and they sink deeper into materialism, into a life that depends on the senses. When they have enough intellect, they even start to believe that theories about the immortality of the body are absolute truths.

The things in the universe that are temporary can never become permanent, and what is permanent can never disappear.

People cannot make the flesh immortal.

June Sixteenth.

All of nature, in its many forms of life, is always changing, temporary, and never lasting. Only the guiding Principle behind nature is permanent. Nature is many things, marked by separation, while the guiding Principle is one, marked by unity. By overcoming the desires of the senses and the selfishness within, which is the act of overcoming nature, a person rises above the personal illusions and steps into the glorious light of the impersonal, the realm of Truth, from which all temporary forms emerge.

So, let people practice self-denial. Let them overcome their animal desires. Let them refuse to be controlled by luxury and pleasure. Let them practice virtue and grow daily into higher and higher virtue until they grow into the Divine.

Only by reaching the God-like state of consciousness can a person enter into immortality.

True service is forgetting oneself in love for all.

June Seventeenth.

Whoever constantly fights against their own selfishness and works to replace it with all-embracing love is a saint, whether they live in a humble home or among wealth and power, whether they preach or live in obscurity.

To the worldly person who is starting to aspire toward higher things, a saint like the gentle St. Francis of Assisi or the determined St. Anthony is a glorious and inspiring sight. To the saint, an equally inspiring sight is the sage, sitting calm and holy, having conquered sin and sorrow, no longer troubled by regret or remorse, and beyond the reach of temptation. Even the sage, however, is drawn to an even more glorious vision—that of the Savior, showing His knowledge through selfless works and using His divinity to bring good by immersing Himself in the suffering heart of humanity.

Only work that is impersonal can last.

Wherever duties, no matter how humble, are done without self-interest and with joyful sacrifice, there is true service and lasting work.

June Eighteenth.

The world has been given one great and divine lesson—the lesson of absolute unselfishness. The saints, sages, and saviors of all times are the ones who have devoted themselves to this task, learned it, and lived it. All the scriptures of the world are written to teach this one lesson, and all the great teachers repeat it. It is too simple for the world, which, rejecting it, stumbles along the complicated paths of selfishness.

To seek this righteousness is to walk the path of Truth and Peace, and whoever enters this path will soon see the Immortality that is beyond birth and death. They will realize that in the divine system of the universe, even the smallest effort is not wasted. The world will not complete its long journey until every soul has entered into the joyful realization of its own divinity.

A pure heart is the goal of all religion and the beginning of divinity.

In the external world, there is constant chaos, change, and unrest, but at the heart of all things, there is perfect peace. In this deep silence dwells the Eternal.

June Nineteenth.

Just as there are depths in the ocean that the strongest storms can never reach, there are quiet, holy depths in the heart of a person that the storms of sin and sorrow can never disturb. To reach this silence and live in it consciously is peace.

Discord may fill the outer world, but at the heart of the universe, unbroken harmony reigns. The human soul reaches out, often blindly, toward the harmony of the sinless state, and to live in this state consciously is peace.

Step away for a while from external things, from the pleasures of the senses, from intellectual arguments, from the noise and excitement of the world, and withdraw into the innermost chamber of your heart. There, free from all selfish desires, you will find a holy calm, a blissful rest. The flawless eye of Truth will open within you, and you will see things as they really are.

Become as little children.

Hatred separates human lives, encourages persecution, and drives nations into merciless war.

June Twentieth.

People cry for peace, but there is no peace, only discord, unrest, and conflict. Without the wisdom that comes from self-renunciation, there can be no true and lasting peace.

The peace that comes from social comfort, temporary pleasures, or worldly success is short-lived and disappears when faced with hardship. Only the Peace of Heaven lasts through all trials, and only the selfless heart can experience the Peace of Heaven.

Holiness is the only undying peace. Self-control leads to it, and the ever-growing Light of Wisdom guides the pilgrim on their way. A person begins to experience this peace as soon as they start walking the path of virtue, but it is only fully realized when self disappears in a life of perfect purity.

This inner peace, this silence, this harmony, this love is the Kingdom of Heaven.

Realize the Light that never fades.

June Twenty-first.

If, dear reader, you wish to experience the Joy that never ends and the peace that cannot be disturbed—if you want to leave behind your sins, sorrows, anxieties, and worries forever—then conquer yourself. Bring every thought, every impulse, every desire into perfect obedience to the divine power within you. There is no other way to peace, and if you refuse to walk this path, all your prayers and rituals will be in vain, and neither gods nor angels can help you. Only the one who overcomes is given the white stone of the new life, on which is written the New and Unknowable Name.

The holy place within you is your true and eternal self—it is the divine within you.

Spiritual Principles can only be gained through long discipline in the pursuit and practice of Virtue.

June Twenty-Second.

A schoolteacher doesn't try to teach a student complex math principles right from the start. The teacher knows that this approach would make learning impossible. Instead, they start with a very simple math problem, explain it, and let the student work on it. After repeated failures and renewed effort, the student finally solves it correctly, and then a harder problem is given, followed by another and another. Only after years of diligent practice does the teacher begin to reveal the deeper principles behind the math.

In the same way, practice always comes before knowledge, even in everyday life. In spiritual matters, in living a higher life, this rule is unchangeable.

Truth can only be reached by daily and hourly practice of the lessons of Virtue.

June Twenty-third.

In a well-ordered home, a child is first taught to be obedient and to behave properly in all situations. The child isn't told why they must do this at first but is simply required to do it. Only after they have succeeded in behaving correctly are they told why it is important. No parent would try to teach their child the principles of morality before requiring them to practice respectful behavior and social responsibility.

Virtue can only be known through action, and the knowledge of Truth can only be gained by perfecting oneself in the practice of Virtue. To be complete in the practice and understanding of Virtue is to be complete in the knowledge of Truth.

Do not be discouraged by failure but be strengthened by difficulties.

Learn the lessons of Virtue, and through them, build up the strength of knowledge, destroying ignorance and the suffering of life.

June Twenty-fourth.

Where Love is, God is. Where Goodness lives, Christ is present. Whoever strives daily against selfishness, shaping their mind toward Truth and Purity, will surely find the Master's presence in their heart. God will be one with the person who overcomes themselves and makes their life God-like and holy, banishing strife, letting go of hate and anger, and leaving behind greed, pride, and desires of the flesh that lie to God and Goodness.

Great will be their peace, and they will find lasting freedom from pain and sorrow by conquering sin. God comes to the pure heart and lives within it. Only the person who walks the Path of Good finds the Life that is hidden with Christ in God.

"Make your heart pure, and you will make your life rich, sweet, and beautiful, untouched by strife."

Keep your mind alert and thoughtful.

June Twenty-fifth.

The first step in disciplining the mind is overcoming laziness. This is the easiest step, but until it is fully achieved, the other steps cannot be taken. Clinging to laziness creates a complete barrier to the Path of Truth. Laziness includes giving the body more rest and sleep than it needs, procrastinating, and neglecting the tasks that need immediate attention. This state of mind must be overcome by waking up early, giving the body only the sleep it needs, and doing every task and duty, no matter how small, promptly and energetically as it comes up.

The heart must be purified of sensual desires and cravings.

A lazy mind cannot achieve any kind of success.

June Twenty-sixth.

Success comes from quietly focusing on a specific goal. It is rooted in personal traits or a combination of them, not in a particular situation or set of circumstances. Circumstances do play a role, but they are useless without the mind that can recognize and make use of them.

At the heart of every success is some form of well-directed energy. There has been a persistent focus on a goal. Success is like a flower— it may seem to bloom suddenly, but it is the result of a long series of efforts and preparation. People see the success, but they don't see the preparation, the many mental processes that led up to it.

Without effort, nothing can be achieved.

To achieve the higher forms of success, a person must give up anxiety, rushing, and fussing.

June Twenty-seventh.

Persistently moving forward along a certain path is sure to lead to a destination that is directly related to that path. Frequently straying off the path or turning back will make all effort useless, and no destination will be reached; success will remain far away.

Effort, more effort, and then even more effort is the key to success. As the simple saying goes:

"If at first you don't succeed, try again." All the advice from successful business people and wise teachers is advice about action. To stop acting is to stop being useful in the flow of life. Action requires effort and exertion.

Transform the energy that wears you down into the deeper, quieter kind that preserves and builds you up.

The quiet, calm people will experience a more lasting form of success than those who are loud and restless.

June Twenty-eighth.

When a person exchanges copper for silver, and silver for gold, they don't stop using money. They just trade a heavier, bulkier form for a smaller, lighter, and more valuable one. In the same way, when a person trades rushing for carefulness, and carefulness for calmness, they don't stop making an effort. They simply exchange a scattered and less effective energy for a more focused, effective, and valuable one.

Even the roughest forms of effort are necessary at first, because without them, the higher forms cannot be developed. A child must crawl before it can walk, it must babble before it can talk, and it must talk before it can compose. A person begins in weakness and ends in strength, but they advance through the effort they put forth.

The root of success is in character.

The same law that punishes us also protects us.

June Twenty-ninth.

When people, in their ignorance, try to destroy themselves, the arms of Divine Love surround them in protective care, even if that protection sometimes comes with pain. Every pain we suffer brings us closer to understanding Divine Wisdom. Every blessing we enjoy reminds us of the perfection of the Great Law and the complete happiness that will be ours when we inherit divine knowledge. We grow by learning, and we learn, up to a certain point, through suffering. When the heart is softened by love, the law of love is understood in all its wonderful kindness. When wisdom is gained, peace is guaranteed.

We cannot change the law of the universe, which is perfect, but we can change ourselves to better understand its perfection and make its greatness our own.

Trying to bring perfection down to the level of imperfection is the height of foolishness, but striving to raise imperfection up to the level of perfection is the height of wisdom.

The wise do not mourn over the order of things.

June Thirtieth.

The wise see the universe as a perfect whole, not as a chaotic mess of parts. The Great Teachers are people of constant joy and heavenly peace.

The blind prisoner of unholy desires may cry out:

"Ah! Love, if you and I could join with Him to fix this sorry scheme of things, wouldn't we break it into pieces and rebuild it closer to what we desire?"

This is the wish of those who seek forbidden pleasures without wanting to face the consequences. These are the people who see the universe as a "sorry scheme of things." They want the universe to conform to their desires and wishes. They seek lawlessness, not law.

But the wise person bends their will and their desires to the Divine Order and sees the universe as the glorious perfection of countless interconnected parts.

To see this is the blessed vision; to know this is the blessed joy.

Wisdom is the goal of every philosophy.

July First.

In any situation, a person can always find the Truth. But they can only find it by using their current condition to become stronger and wiser. Let go of the weak desire for rewards and the fear of punishment, and instead, joyfully commit yourself to doing your duties faithfully. Forget about yourself and your fleeting pleasures, and live a life that is strong, pure, and self-sufficient. By doing this, you will surely find unshakable wisdom, godlike patience, and strength. "No situation exists where there isn't a duty or an ideal to pursue." Everything that is beautiful and blessed is inside you, not in someone else's wealth. Are you poor? You are truly poor if you aren't stronger than your poverty. Have you faced hardships? Tell me, will you solve your troubles by worrying about them? There is no evil that will not disappear if you wisely confront it.

102

Can you fix a broken vase by crying over it?

The power of meekness!

July Second

A person who conquers others by force is strong, but the one who conquers themselves through meekness is truly powerful. A person who conquers another by force will also be conquered, but someone who conquers themselves through meekness will never be defeated, for the human cannot defeat the divine. The meek person triumphs even in defeat. Socrates lives on even more through his death; the crucified Jesus reveals the risen Christ; and Stephen, while being stoned, proves the power of gentleness over stones. What is real cannot be destroyed—only what is false can be. When a person finds what is real within them, something that is constant, unchanging, and eternal, they enter into that reality and become meek. All the forces of darkness may come against them, but they will not be harmed and will eventually be left in peace.

Meekness is a divine quality, and it is all-powerful.

Nothing is hidden from the one who conquers themselves.

July Third

You will penetrate the cause of all causes, lifting one veil of illusion after another until you reach the very heart of existence. By becoming one with Life, you will know all life, and in seeing into causes and understanding realities, you will no longer worry about yourself, others, or the world. Instead, you will see that everything is part of the Great Law. Covered by gentleness, you will bless when others curse; love when others hate; forgive when others condemn; yield when others fight; give up when others hold on; and lose when others seek to gain. In their strength, they will be weak, and in your weakness, you will be strong. Yes, you will prevail. "When Heaven saves a person, it wraps them in gentleness."

He who does not have unbroken gentleness does not have Truth.

How can you fear anyone when you wrong no one?

July Fourth

The righteous person is unbeatable. No enemy can defeat or confuse them, and they need no other protection than their own integrity and holiness. Just as evil cannot defeat good, the righteous cannot be brought down by the unrighteous. Slander, envy, hatred, and malice cannot harm them, nor cause them suffering, and those who try to hurt them only end up bringing shame upon themselves.

The righteous person has nothing to hide, does nothing that requires secrecy, and harbors no thoughts or desires they would be ashamed for others to know. They are fearless and have nothing to hide. Their step is firm, their posture is upright, and their speech is clear and honest. They look everyone in the eye. How can they be ashamed of anything when they deceive no one?

When you stop doing wrong, you cannot be wronged. When you stop deceiving, you cannot be deceived.

The universe is held together because love is at its core.

July Fifth

The Children of Light, who live in the Kingdom of Heaven, see the universe and everything in it as the expression of one Law—the Law of Love. They see Love as the power that shapes, sustains, protects, and perfects everything, both living and non-living. To them, Love is not just a rule to live by; it is the law of life itself. Knowing this, they live their lives according to Love, not thinking about their own desires.

By obeying this divine Love, they become aware participants in its power and reach perfect freedom as Masters of Destiny. Love is pure harmony, pure joy, and contains no element of suffering. Let a person think no thought and do no action that isn't in line with pure Love, and suffering will no longer trouble them.

Love is the only power that preserves.

To know Love is to know that there is no harmful power in the universe.

July Sixth

If someone wants to know Love and experience its eternal joy, they must practice it in their heart. They must become Love. The person who always acts from the spirit of Love is never abandoned and never faces an unsolvable problem because impersonal Love is both knowledge and power. Someone who has learned how to love has learned how to master every difficulty, turn every failure into success, and dress every event and circumstance in beauty and blessing.

The path to Love is through self-mastery, and by walking this path, a person builds their knowledge as they go. When they reach Love, they take full control of their body and mind through the divine power they have earned. "Perfect Love drives out fear."

Perfect Love is perfect harmlessness. And the person who has removed all thoughts of harm and all desires to harm others receives universal protection.

Through self-enlightenment, Perfect Freedom is found.

July Seventh

There is no bondage in the Heavenly Life. There is Perfect Freedom. This is its greatest glory. This Supreme Freedom can only be gained through obedience. The person who obeys the Highest works with the Highest and so masters every force within themselves and every situation outside themselves. A person can choose the lower and ignore the Higher, but the Higher is never defeated by the lower. In this lies the revelation of Freedom. Let a person choose the Higher and let go of the lower, and they will establish themselves as an overcomer and experience Perfect Freedom.

To give in to your desires is the only real slavery; to conquer yourself is the only real freedom. The person who is a slave to self loves their chains and refuses to break them, fearing they would lose some cherished pleasure. In doing this, they defeat and enslave themselves.

The Land of Perfect Freedom is reached through the Gate of Knowledge.

A person will be free when they are freed from themselves.

July Eighth

All outward oppression is only the shadow and result of the true oppression within. For centuries, the oppressed have cried out for freedom, and thousands of man-made laws have failed to provide it. They can only give themselves freedom, and they will only find it by following the Divine Laws written in their hearts. Let them seek inward Freedom, and the shadow of oppression will no longer darken the world. Let people stop oppressing themselves, and no one will oppress their brother. People make laws for outward freedom but continue to make true freedom impossible by maintaining an inner condition of slavery. In this way, they chase after shadows and ignore the reality within. All forms of outward bondage and oppression will disappear when people stop willingly enslaving themselves to passion, error, and ignorance.

Freedom belongs to the free!

The True, the Beautiful, and the Great are always childlike, fresh, and young.

July Ninth

The great person is always the good person; they are always simple. They live in the endless well of divine Goodness within; they dwell in the Heavenly Places; they commune with the great ones who have passed on; they live with the Invisible. They are inspired and breathe the air of Heaven. Whoever wants to be great must first learn to be good. They will become great by not seeking greatness. Aiming at greatness, a person finds nothingness; aiming at nothingness, they find greatness. The desire to be great shows smallness, personal vanity, and selfishness. The willingness to disappear from view and the complete absence of self-promotion is the mark of true greatness. Smallness seeks and loves authority. True greatness is never bossy, and because of that, it becomes the authority to which future generations look.

Be your simple self, your better self, the impersonal self, and you will be great!

The greatness that is flawless, complete, and perfect is beyond all art.

July Tenth

Do you want to teach the living Word? You must give up yourself and become that Word. You must know one thing—that the human heart is good and divine. You must live one thing—Love. You must love all, see no evil, and believe no evil. Then, even if you say little, your every action will be powerful, and your every word will be a lesson. Through your pure thoughts and selfless deeds, even if they seem hidden, you will teach and inspire countless souls for ages to come.

To the one who chooses Goodness, sacrificing everything else, is given all things. They gain the best, commune with the Highest, and join the company of the Great.

The greatness that is flawless, perfect, and complete is beyond all art. It is the manifestation of perfect Goodness. That's why the greatest souls are always Teachers.

Every natural law has a spiritual counterpart.

July Eleventh

Thoughts are like seeds, which, when they fall into the soil of the mind, sprout and grow until they become fully developed. They blossom into actions—good or bad, brilliant or foolish—depending on their nature, and then they become seeds again to be planted in other minds. A teacher is a sower of seeds, a spiritual gardener, while the person who teaches themselves is a wise farmer of their own mind. The growth of a thought is like the growth of a plant. The seed must be sown at the right time, and it takes time for it to develop into the plant of knowledge and the flower of wisdom.

The visible world reflects the invisible.

Energy must not only be directed toward good ends, it must be carefully controlled and conserved.

July Twelfth

The advice of one of the great Teachers to his followers—"Stay wide awake"—perfectly expresses the need for tireless energy if one's goals are to be achieved. It's equally good advice for the salesperson and the saint. "Constant vigilance is the price of freedom," and freedom comes from achieving your goals. The same Teacher said: "If anything is to be done, let a person do it at once; let them tackle it vigorously!" The wisdom of this advice becomes clear when we remember that action is creative, and growth and development follow from proper use. To gain more energy, we must fully use the energy we already have. Only the person who tackles a task with full effort will find power and freedom.

Noise and rushing are just wasted energy.

It's a great mistake to think noise means power.

July Thirteenth

Where there is calmness, there is the greatest power. Calmness shows a strong, well-trained, and disciplined mind. The calm person knows their business, without a doubt. Their words may be few, but they carry weight. Their plans are well thought out, and they work smoothly like a well-oiled machine. They can see far ahead and make straight for their goal. The enemy, Difficulty, becomes a friend because they've learned how to "agree with their adversary along the way." Like a wise general, they've anticipated every challenge. In fact, they are prepared for anything. Through meditation and careful thinking, they've considered every cause and understood how things will likely unfold. They are never caught by surprise, never in a rush, and they remain grounded and steady.

Working steam is quiet. It's the escaping steam that makes all the noise.

Energy is the first pillar in the temple of prosperity.

July Fourteenth

Calmness, unlike the dead stillness of laziness, is the peak of focused energy. There is a strong, concentrated mind behind it. In excitement and agitation, the mind is scattered, weak, and without impact. The fussy, irritable person has no influence. They push others away rather than drawing them in. They wonder why their "easy-going" neighbor is successful and well-liked, while they, who are always rushing and worrying (thinking they are working hard), fail and are avoided. Their neighbor, being a calmer and more deliberate person, gets more work done, does it more skillfully, and is more composed. This is why they are successful and influential. Their energy is focused and used wisely, while the other person's energy is scattered and wasted.

No energy means no ability.

The spendthrift can never become rich, and if they start with riches, they will soon become poor.

The spendthrift can never become rich, but, if he begin with riches, must soon become poor.

July Fifteenth.

The poor person who wants to become rich must start from the bottom and not try to look wealthy by attempting something beyond their means. There's always plenty of room at the bottom, and it's a safe place to start because there's nothing below you and everything above. Many young businesspeople fail because they show off and pretend, thinking that's necessary for success. But this only fools themselves and leads to failure. A modest and honest beginning, in any area, will secure success more than exaggerating one's position or importance.

The thrifty and careful person is on the path to riches.

July Sixteenth

Wearing flashy clothes and jewelry shows an empty, shallow mind. Modest and refined people dress simply, and they use their extra money to further improve their education and character. To them, learning and growth are more important than unnecessary fancy clothing, and they support literature, art, and science. True refinement is in the mind and behavior, and a mind filled with virtue and intelligence cannot be made more attractive by showing off the body, though it may be made less attractive.

Simplicity in dress, as in other things, is best.

Money wasted can be replaced; health wasted can be regained; but time wasted can never be restored.

July Seventeenth

The person who gets up early to think, plan, and reflect will always show more skill and success in their work than the person who stays in bed until the last minute, only getting up in time for breakfast. Spending an hour before breakfast this way is extremely valuable for making your efforts more effective. It helps to calm and clear the mind, focusing your energy to make it more powerful and efficient. The best and most lasting success is often achieved before eight in the morning. The person who starts work at six will always—if all else is equal—be far ahead of the person still in bed at eight.

The day isn't made longer for anyone.

July Eighteenth

There is one right way to do everything, even the smallest thing, and a thousand wrong ways. Skill means finding the one right way and sticking to it. The inefficient person fumbles around, trying the wrong ways, and even when the right way is shown to them, they don't follow it. Sometimes, they do this because they think, in their ignorance, that they know better, which puts them in a position where they can't learn—even if it's something as simple as cleaning a window or sweeping a floor. Thoughtlessness and inefficiency are far too common.

There is always room in the world for people who are thoughtful and efficient. Employers know how hard it is to find the best workers. A good worker, whether with tools or ideas, with words or thoughts, will always have a place to use their skill.

Skill is gained through careful thinking and attention.

There are no shortcuts to success.

July Nineteenth

Just like a bubble can't last, neither can fraud lead to real success. Someone may make a quick, intense effort to get money through dishonest means, but they will eventually fail. Nothing gained through fraud can be kept; it will be returned with a heavy cost. But fraud isn't just practiced by obvious swindlers. Anyone who tries to get money without offering something of equal value in return is committing fraud, whether they realize it or not. People who are always scheming to get rich without working for it are mentally close to thieves, and they eventually come under the influence of such people, losing whatever wealth they have.

True prosperity must be earned through both intelligent work and moral strength.

Integrity is valuable wherever it's found and leaves its mark on everything.

July Twentieth

To be complete and strong, integrity must cover every part of a person's life, extending to even the smallest details. It must be so thorough and lasting that no temptation can cause them to compromise. Failing in one area means failing in all, and giving in to even the smallest lie or dishonesty, no matter how insignificant it seems, is like throwing away the shield of integrity and leaving yourself open to attacks of evil.

The person who works just as carefully when their boss isn't watching as when they are will not stay in a lower position for long. Such integrity in doing their work will quickly lead them to prosperity.

A person of integrity is aligned with the fixed laws of life. They are like a strong tree whose roots are fed by constant springs, and no storm can knock them down.

Ignorant people think dishonesty is a shortcut to success.

July Twenty-first

Honesty is the surest way to succeed. The day will come when the dishonest person regrets their actions in pain and suffering, but no one ever needs to regret being honest. Even when an honest person fails— and they might, if they lack other qualities like energy, thrift, or organization—their failure is never as painful as it is for a dishonest person, because they can always find peace in knowing they never cheated anyone. Even in their darkest moments, they have the comfort of a clear conscience.

A dishonest person is morally short-sighted.

Strong people have strong goals, and strong goals lead to strong achievements.

July Twenty-second

Invincibility is a glorious protector, but it only covers the person whose integrity is pure and unbreakable. Never violating even the smallest principle makes you invincible against all attacks of gossip, slander, or false accusations. But if a person fails in one area, they become vulnerable, and just like Achilles' heel, one small weakness can bring them down. Perfect integrity protects against all attacks and harm, giving its possessor the courage and peace of mind to face all opposition. No amount of talent, intellect, or business skill can provide the peace of mind and strength that come from living by high moral principles.

Moral strength is the greatest power.

A person's true character is revealed by their actions, not by their words.

July Twenty-third

Sympathy should not be confused with shallow emotion, which, like a pretty flower with no roots, soon fades and leaves no lasting impact. Crying uncontrollably when parting with a friend or hearing about distant suffering isn't sympathy. Neither is getting angrily upset over injustice a sign of a truly sympathetic heart. If someone is cruel at home—nagging their spouse, beating their children, or mistreating their servants—yet claims to care about the suffering of people outside their reach, their love is false. Shallow emotion is behind their bursts of outrage over injustice, and it's their own cruelty that shows their true nature.

Sympathy is a deep, unspoken tenderness, shown through a consistently kind and selfless character.

Lack of sympathy comes from selfishness; sympathy comes from love.

July Twenty-fourth

Sympathy connects us to the hearts of others so that we feel their pain and share in their joy. When others are despised or persecuted, we spiritually stand with them in their humiliation and distress. Someone with true sympathy will never be cynical or judgmental and will never pass cruel or thoughtless judgments on others. Their tender heart is always with others in their suffering.

But to reach this deep level of sympathy, a person must have loved deeply, suffered much, and experienced the darkest sorrows. It grows out of these profound experiences, burning away pride, selfishness, and thoughtlessness from the heart.

Sympathy, in its truest sense, is sharing in the struggles and pain of others.

Gentleness is the mark of true spiritual growth.

July Twenty-fifth

Beware of greed, jealousy, suspicion, and envy, because these feelings will rob you of all that is best in life, both in material things and in character and happiness. Be generous in heart and action. Be kind and trusting, not only giving freely of your possessions but also allowing others the freedom to think and act. Live this way, and honor, prosperity, and happiness will come to your door like friends.

Gentleness is close to divinity.

A gentle person—someone whose good behavior comes from thoughtfulness and kindness—is always loved, no matter where they come from.

July Twenty-sixth

A person who has mastered gentleness never argues or fights. They don't respond to harsh words; they either ignore them or answer with kindness, which is far more powerful than anger. Gentleness is united with wisdom, and the wise person has overcome anger in themselves, so they know how to calm it in others. The gentle person avoids many of the conflicts that upset those who can't control themselves. While others exhaust themselves with unnecessary stress, the gentle person remains calm and composed. This calmness helps them succeed in life.

Arguments deal with the surface, but sympathy reaches the heart.

Fake things, whether they are trinkets or people, have no value.

July Twenty-seventh

It's essential to be real. Don't try to appear different from who you are. Don't pretend to have virtues you don't possess or try to adopt qualities you don't have. The hypocrite thinks they can fool the world and the laws of life, but the only person they fool is themselves. For this, the law of life will bring its consequences. There's an old theory that the extremely wicked are destroyed. To be a pretender is to come as close to destruction as a person can, for they lose themselves and are replaced by a shadow of lies.

The person with a sincere heart becomes an example for others: they are more than a person; they are a reality, a force, a guiding principle.

Evil is an experience, not a power.

July Twenty-eighth

The painful experiences of evil fade away as new experiences of goodness take over. And what are these new experiences of goodness? They are many and beautiful: the joyful knowledge of being free from sin; the absence of guilt; freedom from the temptations that once tormented you; incredible joy in situations that used to bring sorrow; the ability to remain unharmed by the actions of others; great patience and sweetness of character; a calm mind in all circumstances; freedom from doubt, fear, and anxiety; and the end of all feelings of dislike, envy, and hostility.

Evil is a state of ignorance and immaturity, and as knowledge grows, evil fades away.

When divine goodness is practiced, life becomes joyful.

July Twenty-ninth

To have the highest virtues is to enjoy the highest happiness. The blessings that Jesus promised are given to those with the greatest virtues: the merciful, the pure in heart, the peacemakers, and so on. Higher virtue doesn't just lead to happiness; it is happiness. It's impossible for a person with the highest virtues to be unhappy. The cause of unhappiness is found in selfishness, not in self-sacrifice. A person can have virtue and still be unhappy, but not if they have divine virtue. Human virtue is mixed with selfishness, and so it brings sorrow, but divine virtue has no trace of selfishness, and with it, all misery is gone.

Truth is beyond and above us.

Where there is passion, there is no peace; where there is peace, there is no passion.

July Thirtieth

People pray for peace but cling to their desires. They create conflict but ask for heavenly rest. This is deep spiritual ignorance. It shows they don't understand the basics of spiritual life. Hatred and love, conflict and peace, cannot exist together in the same heart. Where one is welcomed, the other is pushed out. The person who despises others will be despised in return. The one who fights with others will face resistance. They shouldn't be surprised that people are divided. They should realize they are spreading conflict and understand why they lack peace.

By conquering oneself, Perfect Peace is achieved.

If people only understood That responding to a brother's wrong Shouldn't lead them to another wrong.

July Thirty-first

If people only understood That their wrong doesn't cancel out Another's wrong; That by hating, hate only grows, But by doing good, evil goes, They would cleanse their hearts and actions, Banish all the petty distractions— If they only understood. If people only understood That the heart that sins will feel sorrow, That those with hateful minds tomorrow Reap a barren harvest, weeping, With no rest, no peaceful sleeping, They'd fill their hearts with tenderness, And look with pity at life's mess—

If they only understood. If people only understood How Love conquers . . . They would always Live in love, not hate—if they only understood.

Let a person let go of self, let them overcome the world, let them deny their selfish desires; only by this path can they enter the heart of the Infinite.

August First.

"Goodwill gives insight," and only the person who has conquered their selfishness and has one attitude—goodwill—can have divine understanding and tell the difference between truth and falsehood. The truly good person is, therefore, the wise person, the divine person, the enlightened one who knows the Eternal. Where you find constant gentleness, lasting patience, true humility, kind speech, self-control, selflessness, and deep sympathy, seek that person, for they have realized the Divine. They live with the Eternal and are one with the Infinite. Only those who are spiritually awakened can understand the Universal Reality, where illusions fade away, and dreams and delusions are destroyed.

To center your life in the Great Law of Love is to enter into rest, harmony, and peace.

To understand the Infinite and Eternal is to rise above time.

August Second

To avoid participating in evil and discord, to stop fighting against evil, and to avoid neglecting what is good, while always following the calmness within, is to reach the core of life. This leads to a living, conscious experience of the eternal and infinite principle that remains hidden to the mind alone. Until this principle is understood, the soul is not at peace. Those who understand this are truly wise, not with the knowledge of the learned, but with the simplicity of a pure heart and divine character.

There is one Great Law that demands unconditional obedience, one principle that unites all diversity, and one eternal Truth that makes all earthly problems vanish like shadows.

To understand this Law, Unity, and Truth is to enter the Infinite and become one with the Eternal.

Be rooted in Immortality, Heaven, and the Spirit, which make up the Empire of Light.

August Third

Entering the Infinite is not just a theory or feeling. It is a real experience, the result of constant practice in inner purification. When the body is no longer seen as the true self, when all appetites and desires are completely controlled and purified, when emotions are calm, and the mind is steady, then, and only then, does consciousness become one with the Infinite. It is only then that childlike wisdom and deep peace are achieved.

People grow tired and gray trying to solve life's dark problems, and they die without finding answers because they can't escape the limitations of their personal lives. By trying to save their personal life, they lose the greater, impersonal Life of Truth. By holding on to the temporary, they miss out on the knowledge of the Eternal.

Self and error are one and the same.

August Fourth

Error is tangled in deep complexity, but eternal simplicity is the glory of Truth.

Loving yourself shuts you out from Truth, and by seeking personal happiness, you miss the deeper, purer, lasting joy. As Carlyle said, "There is something higher in man than happiness. He can do without happiness and find blessedness instead... Love not pleasure, love God. This is the Everlasting Yes, where all contradictions are solved, and those who live and work by it are at peace."

The person who has let go of their self, their personality, which most people love and hold on to so tightly, has left behind all confusion and entered a simplicity so deep that the world, caught up in its errors, sees it as foolishness.

At rest in the Infinite.

The realm of Reality is based on unchanging principles.

August Fifth

When a person has given up their lusts, their errors, their opinions, and their prejudices, they enter the knowledge of God. Having given up selfish desires for heaven and the fear of hell, having even given up the love of life itself, they gain supreme joy and Eternal Life, a Life that bridges life and death and knows its own immortality. Having given up everything without holding back, they have gained everything and rest in peace with the Infinite.

Only those who are free from selfishness, who are equally content to be annihilated or to live, are fit to enter the Infinite. Only those who have stopped trusting their temporary self and learned to fully trust the Great Law, the Supreme Good, are ready to experience undying joy.

By giving up self, all difficulties are overcome.

There is no more regret, disappointment, or remorse when selfishness has ended.

August Sixth

The spirit of Love, which is shown in a complete and balanced life, is the crown of existence and the ultimate goal of knowledge on earth. How does a person act when faced with trials and temptations? Many people boast about knowing the Truth, yet they are easily shaken by grief, disappointment, and anger. They crumble under the smallest trial. Truth is unchanging, and to the extent that a person stands on Truth, they become firm in virtue, rise above their passions and emotions, and move beyond their changeable personality.

People create temporary dogmas and call them Truth. But Truth cannot be defined; it is beyond words and the reach of the mind. It can only be experienced through practice and shown in a pure heart and perfect life.

The person who is patient, calm, and forgiving in all circumstances reveals the Truth.

Practice the virtues of the heart and search humbly for the Truth.

August Seventh

Truth cannot be proven by arguments or scholarly essays, because if people do not see Truth in infinite patience, unconditional forgiveness, and universal compassion, no words will ever prove it to them.

It is easy for a person filled with passion to stay calm and patient when everything around them is calm, or when they are alone. It's also easy for a person lacking compassion to be kind when they are treated kindly. But the person who keeps their patience and calm under all trials, who remains gentle and humble even in the most difficult situations, is the only one who possesses the spotless Truth.

Such virtues belong to the Divine and can only be shown by someone who has reached the highest wisdom, who has given up their selfish, passionate nature, and who has realized the unchangeable Law, bringing themselves into harmony with it.

There is one great Law that governs the universe—the Law of Love.

To know the Law of Love, to live in harmony with it, is to become immortal, invincible, and indestructible.

August Eighth

It is through the soul's effort to realize this Law that people come again and again to live, suffer, and die. When the Law is understood, suffering ends, the self is dissolved, and the life and death of the body are destroyed, as consciousness becomes one with the Eternal.

The Law is completely impartial, and its highest expression is Service. When the purified heart understands the Truth, it is called to make the greatest and most sacred sacrifice—the sacrifice of the enjoyment of Truth. Through this sacrifice, the soul, now free, chooses to live among the lowliest, serving all of humanity.

The Spirit of Love is the only force worthy of eternal worship.

Truth cannot be limited.

August Ninth

The glory of the saint, the sage, and the savior is this: they have reached the deepest humility and the greatest unselfishness. Having given up everything, even their own identity, their actions are holy and lasting, free from any trace of selfishness. They give without expecting anything in return; they work without dwelling on the past or worrying about the future and never look for rewards.

When a farmer has tilled the land, planted the seeds, and tended the crops, they know they have done all they can. Now they must trust nature and wait patiently for time to bring the harvest. No amount of waiting or wishing can speed up the result.

In the same way, the person who has realized the Truth sows seeds of goodness, purity, love, and peace without expecting anything in return. They trust the Great Law, which will bring its own harvest in due time. This Law is both the source of creation and destruction.

Every holy person became such through constant self-sacrifice.

The holy path begins with controlling one's passions.

August Tenth

What the saints, sages, and saviors accomplished, you too can accomplish if you walk the same path of self-sacrifice and selfless service. Truth is simple. It says, "Give up self," "Come to Me" (leave behind all that stains your heart), and "I will give you rest." All the many explanations and commentaries cannot hide this truth from a heart earnestly seeking righteousness. You don't need learning to know it; you can find it even without knowledge.

Though disguised in many ways by selfish people, the clear and simple nature of Truth remains unchanged.

It is not by creating complicated theories or philosophies that Truth is realized, but by weaving a life of inner purity and building the temple of a spotless life that Truth is found.

Saintliness is the beginning of holiness.

Only when you identify with the Divine can you be truly "clothed and in your right mind."

August Eleventh

The divine within is the home of peace, the temple of wisdom, and the dwelling place of immortality. Without this inner resting place, this place of vision, there can be no real peace or knowledge of the Divine. And if you can remain there for a minute, an hour, or a day, then it's possible for you to stay there forever.

Your sins and sorrows, your fears and anxieties, are your own, and you can hold on to them, or you can let them go. You cling to your unrest by choice, and by choice, you can find lasting peace. No one can give up sin for you; you must give it up yourself. The greatest Teacher can only walk the path of Truth for themselves and show it to you. You must walk it for yourself.

Freedom and peace come only through your efforts, by giving up what binds your soul and takes away your peace.

Give up all selfishness, and the Peace of God will be yours.

Leave the storms of sin and anguish behind.

August Twelfth

O you who would teach men of Truth!
Have you passed through the desert of doubt?
Have you been purified by the fires of sorrow?
Have you cast out the demons of opinion
From your human heart?
Is your soul so pure
That no false thought can live there?
O you who would teach men of Love!
Have you crossed the place of despair?
Have you cried through the long night of grief?
Is your heart,
Now freed from sorrow and care,
Moved with pity
When you see wrong, hate, and suffering?
O you who would teach men of Peace!
Have you crossed the wide sea of conflict?
Have you found, on the shores of silence, freedom
From the restless struggles of life?
Has all your striving
Faded from your heart,
Leaving only Truth, Love, and Peace?
Enter the resting place within.

Make yourself pure and loving, and you will be loved by all.

August Thirteenth

Think of those who serve you with kindness, consider their happiness
and comfort, and never demand from them what you would not be
willing to do yourself. Rare and beautiful is the humility of a servant
who forgets themselves for the good of their master, but even rarer

and more beautiful is the nobility of a person who forgets their own happiness and seeks the happiness of those under their care. Such a person's happiness is increased many times over, and they rarely need to complain about those they employ.

A well-known employer once said, "I've always had the best relationship with my workers. If you ask me how, I can only say that I've always tried to treat them as I would want to be treated."

Be kind to others, and friends will soon surround you.

Living with good thoughts creates an atmosphere of sweetness and power that touches everyone who meets you.

August Fourteenth

Just as the rising sun drives away the shadows, so all the powerless forces of evil are driven away by the positive thoughts that shine from a heart strong in purity and faith.

Where there is strong faith and unwavering purity, there is health, success, and power. In such a person, disease, failure, and disaster find no place to grow because there is nothing to feed them.

Even physical health is largely shaped by mental attitudes, and the scientific world is starting to recognize this truth. The old belief that a person is shaped by their body is fading, replaced by the inspiring idea that the mind controls the body, and the body is shaped by the power of thought.

There is no evil in the universe that doesn't begin in the mind.

August Fifteenth.

If you are prone to anger, worry, jealousy, greed, or any other negative state of mind, and still expect perfect physical health, you are asking for the impossible because you are constantly planting the seeds of illness in your mind. Wise people avoid these harmful thoughts because they know they are more dangerous than a bad environment or an unhealthy home. If you want to be free from physical aches and pains and experience perfect health, you must first put your mind in order and align your thoughts. Think joyful, loving thoughts; let the spirit of goodwill flow through you like medicine, and you will need nothing else. Get rid of your jealousy, suspicions, worries, hatreds, and selfish habits, and you will get rid of your indigestion, stress, anxiety, and aching joints.

If you want to stay healthy, you must learn to work without unnecessary tension.

Organize your thoughts, and you will organize your life.

August Sixteenth

Pour the oil of peace over the stormy waters of your emotions and prejudices, and no matter how much misfortune threatens, it will not be able to wreck your soul as it journeys through life. If your soul is guided by a cheerful and unshakeable faith, your path will be even more secure, and many dangers will pass you by that might otherwise cause harm. Through the power of faith, every lasting achievement is accomplished. Faith in the Supreme; faith in the law that governs everything; faith in your work and your ability to accomplish it—this is the foundation upon which you must build if you wish to succeed and remain standing through challenges.

Always follow the highest inner voice, no matter the circumstances.

Let your heart become large, loving, and selfless, and your influence and success will grow and endure.

August Seventeenth

Develop a pure and selfless spirit, and combine that with faith and a clear purpose, and you will build lasting success, greatness, and power.

If you are unhappy in your current situation, and your heart is not in your work, still perform your duties with care and diligence. Keep in mind that a better position and greater opportunities are waiting for you, and always be mentally prepared for new possibilities. When the right moment arrives, and a new path presents itself, you will be ready to step into it with confidence, foresight, and the discipline you've developed.

Whatever task you are given, focus your whole mind on it and put in all your energy. Completing small tasks with excellence will eventually lead to bigger responsibilities.

Learn, through practice, how to manage your energy and focus it at the right time.

Passion is not power; it is the misuse and scattering of power.

August Eighteenth

When that young man I knew faced constant setbacks and misfortunes and was mocked by his friends who told him to give up, he replied, "The time is near when you will marvel at my success and good fortune." He showed that he possessed that quiet and unstoppable strength that eventually led him to overcome countless difficulties and succeed in life.

If you don't have this strength, you can develop it through practice, and the beginning of strength is also the beginning of wisdom. Start by overcoming the small, meaningless things that you've been letting control you. Excessive laughter, gossip, idle talk, and joking just to entertain others—these habits must be set aside as they waste valuable energy.

Focus on one goal; have a clear and useful purpose, and commit yourself to it fully.

True happiness is the deep inner state of complete satisfaction, which is joy and peace.

August Nineteenth

The satisfaction that comes from fulfilling your desires is short-lived and often misleading. It is quickly followed by an even greater need for more. Desire is as endless as the ocean, and it demands more and more as you try to satisfy it. It consumes those who follow it until they are left in physical or mental pain, and they are forced to go through the fires of suffering to be purified. Desire is the gateway to suffering, and all pain stems from it. Letting go of desire leads to the realization of peace, and all true joy awaits the one who reaches that state.

As the poem goes:
"I sent my soul through the invisible,
Some letter of that afterlife to spell,
And by and by my soul returned to me,
And whispered, 'I myself am heaven and hell.'"
Heaven and hell are states of mind.
Seeking selfishly only leads to the loss of happiness.

August Twentieth

When you sink into selfishness and its pleasures, you sink into hell. When you rise above selfishness and forget yourself, you enter heaven. Selfishness is blind, without wisdom, and always leads to suffering. Clear thinking, fair judgment, and true knowledge belong only to the divine state, and only as you enter this divine consciousness can you know what real happiness is. As long as you keep selfishly seeking your own happiness, it will slip further away from you, and you will be sowing seeds of misery. The more you forget yourself in helping others, the more happiness will come to you, and you will harvest peace and joy.

Lasting happiness will come to you when you stop clinging selfishly and are willing to give up.

Whatever you constantly think about, you will come to understand and become more like.

August Twenty-first

Spiritual meditation is the path to divinity. It's the mystical ladder that stretches from earth to heaven, from mistakes to truth, from suffering to peace. Every saint has climbed it, every sinner will eventually have to, and every weary soul that turns away from selfishness and the world and looks toward the Father's Home must place their feet on its golden steps. Without meditation, you cannot grow into the divine state, or experience divine peace, and the eternal joy and truth will remain hidden from you.

If you dwell on selfish and corrupt thoughts, you will become selfish and corrupt.

If you want to enter the deep and lasting peace, start now by meditating.

August Twenty-second

Choose a time of day to meditate, and make it sacred to that purpose. The best time is early morning when everything is calm and peaceful. At this time, all the natural conditions will work in your favor. After a night's rest, your body's passions will be calm, and the worries and stress of the previous day will have faded. Your mind, strong yet relaxed, will be ready to receive spiritual guidance. One of the first challenges you will face is overcoming laziness and self-indulgence. If you refuse, you won't be able to progress, because spiritual growth demands discipline.

The lazy and indulgent cannot know the truth.

The result of your meditations will be a calm spiritual strength.

August Twenty-third

If you are prone to hatred or anger, meditate on gentleness and forgiveness so you can become more aware of how foolish and harmful your behavior is. Then begin to focus on thoughts of love, kindness, and abundant forgiveness. As you overcome the lower by the higher, you will gradually gain an understanding of the divine Law of Love and how it applies to all areas of life and behavior. By applying this knowledge to your thoughts, words, and actions, you will grow gentler, more loving, and more divine. Every fault, every selfish desire, every human weakness can be overcome by the power of meditation. As each sin and mistake is removed, a greater light of Truth will shine on your soul.

Holy thought has great power to overcome.

Meditation will fill your soul with wisdom during times of struggle, sorrow, or temptation.

August Twenty-fourth

As you grow in wisdom through meditation, you will let go of your selfish desires, which are fleeting and cause pain and sorrow. You will stand more firmly on unchanging principles and experience heavenly peace. Meditation leads to knowledge of eternal truths, and the strength gained from meditation helps you trust and live by those truths. The goal of meditation is direct knowledge of Truth, God, and the realization of deep, divine peace.

Rise above selfish devotion to false gods or narrow beliefs; go beyond empty rituals and ignorance.

Remember that you grow into Truth by steady persistence.

Believe that a life of perfect holiness is possible.

August Twenty-fifth

As you believe, aspire, and meditate, your spiritual experiences will become wonderfully sweet and beautiful, and you will receive glorious insights that will fill your soul. As you understand divine Love, divine Justice, and the Perfect Law of Good (God), your joy will deepen, and your peace will grow. The old ways will pass away, and everything will become new. The material world, which once seemed so solid and real, will appear transparent and light to the eyes of Truth. Time will lose its hold on you, and you will live in Eternity. Change and mortality will no longer cause you fear or sorrow because you will be grounded in the unchanging and will live in the heart of immortality.

Those who believe quickly rise to spiritual heights.

Where self is, Truth cannot be; where Truth is, self cannot remain.

August Twenty-sixth

In the human soul, two masters constantly fight for control—the master of self, often called the "Prince of this world," and the master of Truth, often called the Father God. Self is the rebellious master, whose tools are passion, pride, greed, vanity, and selfishness—the tools of darkness. Truth is the humble master, whose tools are gentleness, patience, purity, sacrifice, humility, and love—the tools of Light.

Within every soul, this battle rages, and just as a soldier can't fight for two opposing armies, each heart must serve either self or Truth. There is no middle ground. Jesus, the manifested Christ, said, "No one can serve two masters; either you will hate one and love the other, or you will hold to one and despise the other. You cannot serve both God and money."

You cannot see the beauty of Truth while looking through the eyes of self.

Those who love Truth serve it by sacrificing their selfishness.

August Twenty-seventh

Do you want to know and experience Truth? Then you must be ready to give up everything, for Truth in all its glory can only be seen and known when every trace of self is gone.

Jesus said that whoever would follow him must "deny themselves daily." Are you willing to give up your desires, your prejudices, your opinions? If so, you may begin the narrow path of Truth and find peace, which the world cannot offer. The complete denial of self is the perfect state of Truth, and all religions and philosophies are merely guides to help you reach this supreme goal.

As you let self die, you will be reborn in Truth.

Every holy person is a savior of humanity.

August Twenty-eighth

When people lose their way in selfishness and error, they forget the "heavenly birth," the state of holiness and Truth. They create false standards to judge one another and make their religion the test of Truth, causing endless division, conflict, and suffering.

If you seek to return to the state of Truth, there is only one way: let self die. All the desires, opinions, limited beliefs, and prejudices that you have clung to, let them fall away. No longer let them control you, and Truth will be yours. Stop viewing your religion as superior to others, and strive to learn the supreme lesson of charity.

To live in the world but not be of the world is the highest state of perfection.

The cause of all strength and weakness is within.

August Twenty-ninth

A deep understanding of the Great Law that governs the universe leads to obedience. To know that justice, harmony, and love rule the universe is to understand that all suffering and hardship come from our disobedience to that Law. This knowledge leads to strength and power, and only on this knowledge can a true life, lasting success, and happiness be built. Patience under all circumstances and acceptance of all circumstances as necessary for growth allow you to rise above suffering and overcome it fully, without fear of its return, for through obedience to the Law, it is destroyed.

There is no progress without inner growth.

There is no lasting peace or success without steady advancement in knowledge.

August Thirtieth

Maybe you are weighed down by poverty, friendless and alone, and you wish with all your heart that your burden would be lifted, but it stays, and the darkness around you seems to grow. Perhaps you complain about your situation and blame your birth, your parents, your employer, or the powers that be for unfairly giving you poverty and hardship while others enjoy wealth and ease. Stop complaining and worrying; none of these things are the cause of your poverty. The cause is within you, and where the cause is, there is also the remedy.

There is no room for a complainer in a universe governed by law, and worrying is the death of the soul.

Your thoughts are who you really are.

August Thirty-first

The world around you, whether living or not, takes on the appearance your thoughts give it. "All that we are is the result of what we have thought; it is founded on our thoughts; it is made up of our thoughts." This is what Buddha said, and it follows that if someone is happy, it is because they dwell on happy thoughts. If they are miserable, it's because they focus on negative, weakening thoughts. Whether someone is fearful or brave, foolish or wise, troubled or calm, the cause of their condition lies within their own soul, not outside of it. And now, I hear many voices saying, "Do you really mean to say that circumstances don't affect our minds?" I do not say that, but I know this to be a fact: circumstances can only affect you as much as you allow them to. You are controlled by circumstances only because you don't fully understand the nature, purpose, and power of thought.

Making your happiness depend on your health puts matter above mind, and spirit below the body.

September First.

Men with strong minds do not dwell on their physical condition if it's in any way unwell—they ignore it and continue to work and live as if nothing is wrong. This disregard for the body not only keeps the mind clear and strong, but it is also the best way to help the body heal. Even if we don't have a perfectly healthy body, we can have a healthy mind, and a healthy mind is the best path to physical health.

A sick mind is worse than a sick body because it eventually leads to physical illness. Mental sickness is more pitiful than physical sickness. There are invalids (doctors know them) who just need to lift themselves into a strong, happy, unselfish state of mind to realize their body is actually healthy and capable.

Moral values are the best foundation for both health and happiness.

People are not made unhappy by poverty, but by the desire for wealth.

September Second

Where there is a cause, its effect will follow. If wealth were the cause of immorality, and poverty the cause of corruption, then all rich people would be immoral, and all poor people would be corrupt.

A wrongdoer will do wrong no matter their circumstances— whether they are rich, poor, or somewhere in between. A person who does right will do right no matter where they are. Extreme circumstances may bring out the evil that is already inside, but they cannot create it.

Poverty is often in the mind rather than the wallet. As long as someone craves more money, they will feel poor, and in that sense, they are poor because greed is a form of mental poverty.

A miser may have millions, but he is as poor as he was when he had nothing.

A person is great in knowledge, self-control, and influence based on how well they control themselves.

September Third

The forces in nature are impressive, but they are nothing compared to the intelligent power of the human mind, which controls and directs those natural forces. To understand, control, and direct your inner forces—your desires, will, and thoughts—is to control the destiny of individuals and nations.

A person who understands and controls the forces of nature is a scientist. But someone who understands and controls the forces within the mind is a master of life. The same laws that govern our knowledge of the external world also govern our understanding of the inner self.

The purpose of knowledge is to serve, to improve the world's comfort and happiness.

Everything, whether seen or unseen, follows the infinite and eternal law of cause and effect.

September Fourth

Perfect justice holds the universe together; perfect justice governs human life and behavior. All the different conditions of life that exist today are the result of this law acting on human behavior. A person can choose what actions they take, but they cannot change the nature of the results. They can choose what thoughts to think and what actions to take, but they cannot change the outcomes of those thoughts and actions. These are determined by the higher law.

A person has the power to act, but their power ends once the action is taken. The result cannot be changed, canceled, or escaped. It is unchangeable.

Evil thoughts and actions lead to suffering, while good thoughts and actions lead to happiness.

A person's happiness or misery is determined by their own actions.

September Fifth

Life can be compared to a math problem. To someone who has not yet figured out how to solve it, it seems difficult and confusing. But once they grasp the solution, it becomes as simple as it once seemed impossible. Just like there are countless ways to get a math problem wrong but only one way to get it right, so it is in life. When the right path is found, the confusion disappears, and the person knows they have mastered the problem.

In life, there is no hiding from the truth; the law of the universe exposes everything.

Selfish thoughts and bad actions will not create a useful and beautiful life.

September Sixth

Life is like a piece of fabric, and the individual threads are people's lives. Each thread is independent, but all are connected to form the whole. Every person experiences the consequences of their own actions, not those of others. Each person's path is clear and distinct, creating a complicated but harmonious pattern of actions and reactions, causes and effects. The consequences of each action are always in perfect proportion to the initial act.

Each person creates or destroys their own life.

People are responsible for their actions and the outcomes they bring.

September Seventh

The "problem of evil" exists in a person's own wrong actions, and it is solved when those actions are purified. Rousseau said, "Man, stop searching for the origin of evil; you are its source."

Cause and effect are always linked. Emerson said, "Justice is never delayed; perfect balance is always maintained in life." In a deep sense, cause and effect are immediate and inseparable. As soon as someone thinks a cruel thought, they have harmed their mind. They are not the same person they were a moment before—they are a little more corrupt and a little more miserable. A series of bad thoughts and actions will create a cruel and miserable person.

A kind thought or action instantly brings nobility and happiness.

Without strength of mind, nothing worthy can be accomplished.

September Eighth

Building a stable and firm character, often called "willpower," is one of the most important duties of a person. It is necessary for both their success in life and their inner peace. Having a clear purpose is the foundation of all successful efforts, whether in the physical or spiritual world. Without it, a person will be unhappy and dependent on others for support when they should be self-reliant.

The path to developing willpower is found in the simple, everyday actions of life. It's so obvious that most people overlook it, thinking the answer must be more complicated or mysterious.

The way to grow stronger is to tackle and overcome weaknesses.

The first step in developing willpower is to break free from bad habits.

September Ninth

Those who understand this basic truth will see that the whole process of building willpower can be summed up in these seven rules:

Break bad habits.

Form good habits.

Pay close attention to the task at hand.

Do everything that needs to be done, and do it immediately.

Live by principle.

Control your speech.

Control your thoughts.

Anyone who meditates on and practices these rules will develop the clear purpose and strong will needed to overcome challenges and succeed in difficult situations.

Giving in to bad habits means losing control over yourself.

September Tenth

Those who avoid self-discipline and seek shortcuts to willpower without effort are deceiving themselves and weakening whatever willpower they have.

The strength of will gained by overcoming bad habits allows a person to form good habits. While breaking a bad habit requires willpower, forming a new habit requires intelligent direction. To do this, a person must be mentally active and alert, constantly watching their behavior.

Thoroughness is an essential step in developing willpower and cannot be skipped. Sloppy work shows weakness.

Perfection should be the goal, even in the smallest tasks.

September Eleventh

By not dividing your attention and giving full focus to each task as it arises, you develop single-mindedness and intense concentration. These are two mental strengths that bring both peace and joy to the person who possesses them.

Doing everything that needs to be done immediately and vigorously is just as important. Idleness and a strong will cannot coexist, and procrastination blocks the development of purposeful action. Nothing should be put off, not even for a few minutes. What needs to be done now should be done now. This may seem small, but it is incredibly important. It leads to strength, success, and peace.

Live by principle, not by emotion.

Thoroughness means doing the little things as if they were the most important tasks in the world.

September Twelfth

Understanding the importance of little things is key to success, though many people overlook this truth. Thinking that small tasks can be neglected or done carelessly is the cause of the lack of thoroughness that results in poor work and unhappy lives.

When a person realizes that great things are made up of small things, and that without the small things, the great would not exist, they begin to pay attention to the details they once ignored.

Someone who develops thoroughness becomes useful and influential.

The desire for pleasure is the cause of the common lack of thoroughness.

September Thirteenth

Every employer knows how hard it is to find people who will put thought and energy into their work and do it thoroughly. Poor workmanship is widespread, and few acquire real skill and excellence. Thoughtlessness, carelessness, and laziness are common faults, and it's no wonder that despite efforts at "social reform," the number of unemployed people continues to grow. Those who do poor work today will one day find themselves desperately looking for work without success.

The law of "survival of the fittest" is not based on cruelty, but on justice. It is part of the divine order. If vice were not punished, how could virtue be developed? The lazy and thoughtless cannot take the place of the hardworking and thoughtful.

A mind focused on pleasure cannot also focus on performing duties perfectly.

September Fourteenth

Thoroughness means completeness and perfection. It means doing a task so well that nothing is left unfinished. It means doing your work as well as anyone else, if not better. It involves putting a lot of thought, energy, and persistence into the task and developing patience, perseverance, and a strong sense of duty. An ancient teacher once said, "If something needs to be done, do it, and do it with vigor." Another said, "Whatever your hand finds to do, do it with all your might."

It is better to be fully committed to life than to be half-hearted in religion.

A person who hasn't learned how to be gentle, loving, and happy has learned very little.

September Fifteenth.

Feelings like discouragement, irritability, worry, complaining, and grumbling are like diseases of the mind. They show that something is wrong with your thinking. People who suffer from these should work to improve their thoughts and actions. Yes, there is much sin and suffering in the world, and our love and compassion are needed, but our misery is not. There is already too much misery. What the world needs more of is our cheerfulness and happiness because there is too little of that. The best gift we can give to the world is a beautiful life and character. Without this, everything else is in vain. It is the most important thing—real, lasting, and unshakable, and it includes all joy and blessings.

A man's surroundings are never against him; they are there to help him.

You can change everything around you if you change yourself.

September Sixteenth

A steady, gentle attitude, even in the face of opposition, is a sure sign of a person who has conquered themselves. It shows wisdom and is proof that they possess the Truth.

A kind and joyful soul is the result of wisdom. It spreads its influence invisibly, bringing joy to others and making the world a better place.

If you want others to be honest, be honest. If you want the world to be free from misery and sin, free yourself. If you want your home and surroundings to be happy, be happy.

This will happen naturally as you realize the good within yourself.

Start living free from all wrong and evil. Peace of mind and true change begin here.

Immortality exists right now; it is not just something after death.

September Seventeenth

Immortality doesn't exist in time, and it will never be found there. It belongs to Eternity. Just as time is here and now, so is Eternity, and a person can find that Eternity and establish themselves in it if they overcome the self that clings to the temporary and unsatisfying things of time.

As long as a person is caught up in sensations, desires, and the passing events of daily life, and sees these things as part of who they are, they cannot understand immortality. What this person desires, which they mistake for immortality, is persistence—a continuous series of sensations and events in time.

Persistence is the opposite of immortality.

The death of the body cannot give a person immortality.

September Eighteenth

Spirits are no different from humans. They live a short, restless life with moments of broken awareness, still caught in change and mortality. A mortal person, who craves the continuation of their pleasure-loving personality, remains mortal after death. They simply live another life that has a beginning and an end, without memory of the past or knowledge of the future.

The immortal person is the one who has risen above the things of time and entered a state of consciousness that is constant and unchanging, unaffected by passing events and sensations. This person is like someone who has woken up from a dream. They understand that their dream was not a lasting reality but a fleeting illusion. This person has true knowledge—knowledge of both the temporary state of persistence and the eternal state of immortality.

The immortal person is fully in control of themselves.

The mortal person lives in a state of consciousness that begins and ends.

September Nineteenth

The immortal person stays calm and unshaken through all changes, and the death of their body does not interrupt the eternal consciousness in which they live. It is said of such a person, "They shall not taste of death," because they have stepped out of the stream of mortality and into the Truth. Bodies, personalities, nations, and worlds may pass away, but Truth remains, its glory undimmed by time.

The immortal person is the one who has mastered themselves. They no longer identify with the self-serving forces of personality but have learned to direct those forces with skill and have brought them into harmony with the source of all things.

The immortal person lives in a state of consciousness where there is no beginning or end, only an eternal present.

Overcoming self removes all the sources of sorrow.

September Twentieth

The idea of overcoming or ending the self is very simple. In fact, it is so simple and practical that a five-year-old child could understand it better than many older people, who have lost sight of simple truths by adopting complicated ideas and philosophies.

Overcoming the self means getting rid of all the things inside us that cause division, conflict, suffering, sickness, and sorrow. It does not mean destroying anything good or beautiful.

Overcoming the self means developing all the qualities that are divine.

To defeat the enemy of temptation, you must find where it hides and discover the weaknesses in your own defense where it enters so easily.

September Twenty-first

Temptation, with all its struggles, can be conquered here and now, but it can only be conquered with knowledge. Temptation is a state of darkness or partial darkness. The fully enlightened soul cannot be tempted. When a person fully understands the source, nature, and meaning of temptation, they will overcome it and find rest from their struggles. But as long as they remain in ignorance, no amount of religious practice, prayer, or reading of Scripture will bring them peace.

This is the holy battle of the saints.

All temptation comes from within.

September Twenty-second

People fail to overcome temptation because they often believe two false ideas: first, that all temptations come from outside, and second, that they are tempted because of their goodness. As long as someone is trapped by these beliefs, they will make no progress. When they let go of these beliefs, they will begin to quickly move from victory to victory and experience spiritual joy and peace.

The source of all temptation is the desire within. Once that desire is purified or removed, no outside object or force can tempt the soul. The outside object only provides the opportunity for temptation; it is never the cause. The cause lies in the desire of the person being tempted.

A person is tempted because there are desires or states of mind that they consider to be wrong.

Goodness cannot be tempted. It destroys temptation.

September Twenty-third

It is the bad within a person that is tempted. The level of temptation a person faces reflects the extent of their unholiness. As a person cleanses their heart, temptation disappears. When a wrong desire is removed from the heart, the object that once attracted it can no longer do so. It becomes powerless because there is nothing in the heart to respond to it. An honest person cannot be tempted to steal, no matter how easy the opportunity. A person with pure desires cannot be tempted by gluttony or drunkenness. A person with inner calm and virtue cannot be tempted to anger, and the charms of the immoral have no effect on a purified heart.

Temptation shows a person where they truly stand.

The Great Law is good. The person of integrity is above fear, failure, poverty, shame, and disgrace.

September Twenty-fourth

A person who denies the truth within them because they fear losing comfort or material pleasures can be hurt, robbed, and disgraced because they have first harmed, robbed, and disgraced their own higher self. But a person of steady virtue and unshakable integrity cannot be harmed in this way because they have rejected their cowardly self and taken refuge in Truth.

It is not chains or punishment that make a person a slave, but the fact that they are already a slave to themselves.

Slander, accusations, and malice cannot affect the righteous person or cause them to respond with bitterness. Nor do they need to defend themselves or prove their innocence. Innocence and integrity alone are enough to answer whatever hatred throws at them.

The person of integrity turns all bad things into good.

September Twenty-fifth

The person of integrity should rejoice when they are tested. They should be thankful for the chance to prove their loyalty to the noble values they hold dear. Let them think, "Now is the moment of holy opportunity! Now is the time for Truth to triumph! Even if I lose everything, I will not abandon what is right!" With this attitude, they will respond to evil with good and feel compassion for those who wrong them.

The slanderer, the gossip, and the wrongdoer may seem to succeed for a time, but Justice always wins in the end. The person of integrity may seem to fail for a time, but they are invincible. No force in the world, seen or unseen, can defeat them.

The person of integrity cannot be overcome by darkness, for they have already conquered it within themselves.

September Twenty-sixth

A person's mind and life should be free from confusion. They should be ready to face every difficulty—mental, material, or spiritual—without getting caught in doubt or uncertainty, as many do when troubles or hardships arise. A person should be strong and prepared for any emergency, but this readiness cannot be achieved without the ability to think clearly, and this ability can only be developed through practice and use of the analytical mind.

The mind, like a muscle, grows stronger with use.

Confusion, suffering, and spiritual darkness come from thoughtlessness.

September Twenty-seventh

A person who is afraid to examine their opinions critically or question their beliefs will need to develop moral courage before they can achieve clarity of thought.

A person must be honest with themselves and fearless in facing their own thoughts if they are to discover the pure principles of Truth and receive the Light of Truth.

The more we question Truth, the clearer it becomes. It cannot be harmed by examination or analysis.

The more we question error, the darker it becomes. It cannot survive the light of pure and honest thought.

To "test everything" is to find what is good and reject what is bad.

A person who reasons and meditates learns to see clearly. A person who sees clearly finds the eternal Truth.

Harmony, blessings, and the Light of Truth come to those who think deeply.

September Twenty-eighth

Belief is the foundation of all actions, and because of this, the belief that controls a person's heart or mind is reflected in their life. Every person acts, thinks, and lives in perfect harmony with what they believe deep down. The laws of the mind are so precise that it is impossible for someone to believe in two opposing ideas at once. For example, it is impossible to believe in both justice and injustice, hatred and love, peace and conflict, self-interest and truth at the same time.

Everyone believes in one or the other of these opposites, never in both, and a person's daily actions show what they believe in.

Belief and behavior are connected, for one determines the other.

Justice rules, and what we call injustice is temporary and an illusion.

September Twenty-ninth

The person who constantly complains about the injustice of others or feels they are being mistreated shows by their behavior and attitude that they believe in injustice. No matter what they may say, deep down they believe that confusion and chaos are in charge of the universe. This belief causes them to live in misery and unrest, and their behavior reflects it.

On the other hand, a person who believes in love, in its stability and power, practices love under all circumstances. They remain constant in love, giving it freely to both enemies and friends.

The person who believes in justice stays calm through all challenges and difficulties.

Every thought, action, and habit comes from what a person believes.

September Thirtieth

People are saved from error by believing in the power of Truth. They are saved from sin by believing in Holiness or Perfection. They are saved from evil by believing in Goodness, for every belief is expressed in how we live. It's not necessary to ask about a person's religious beliefs because that's not what matters. What good is it for someone to believe that Jesus died for them or that Jesus is God if they continue to live in sin and wrongdoing? The only question to ask is, "How does this person live?" "How do they act when things get tough?" The answers to these questions reveal whether a person believes in the power of evil or the power of Goodness.

When we stop believing in something, we stop practicing it.

A person cannot hold on to anything unless they believe in it. Belief always comes before action, so a person's actions and life are the results of what they believe.

October First.

Whoever believes in good things will love them and live in them. Whoever believes in impure and selfish things will love them and hold on to them. A tree is known by its fruits.

A person's beliefs about God, Jesus, or the Bible are one thing, but their life—reflected in their actions—is another. Because of this, a person's theological belief doesn't really matter. What matters are the thoughts they keep, their attitude toward others, and their actions. These alone show whether their heart believes in truth or in lies.

There are only two beliefs that truly impact life: belief in good and belief in evil.

Just as a tree produces fruit and a spring flows with water, action is the result of thought.

October Second

When someone falls into a serious sin under great temptation, it may seem like a sudden event. But it is neither sudden nor without cause. If we look closer at the hidden thoughts leading up to it, we can see that the fall was the final outcome of something that started in the mind, perhaps years before. The person allowed a wrong thought to enter their mind, welcomed it a second and third time, and eventually let it settle in their heart. Gradually, they got used to it, nurtured it, and let it grow. Eventually, it became strong enough to bring about the opportunity to act on it.

All sin and temptation are the natural result of a person's thoughts.

Watch your thoughts carefully, for what you think today will eventually shape what you do.

October Third

"There is nothing hidden that will not be revealed," and every thought in your mind must eventually show itself in your actions, whether good or bad. This happens because of the natural laws that guide the universe. The wise teacher and the person driven by pleasure both become who they are based on the thoughts they planted in their hearts, which they then nurtured and cultivated.

No one can overcome sin and temptation by wrestling with opportunities. They can only do so by purifying their thoughts.

A person attracts what is in harmony with their nature.

As a thinking being, your dominant mental attitude shapes your life conditions.

October Fourth

You are the thinker of your thoughts, and because of that, you are also the creator of yourself and your life. Thought causes and creates, showing up in your character and life in the form of results. There are no accidents in your life—its joys and troubles are the echoes of your thoughts. A person thinks, and their life takes shape.

If your dominant mental attitude is peaceful and loving, happiness and blessings will follow you. If your thoughts are resistant and hateful, trouble and distress will cloud your path. From ill will comes grief and disaster; from goodwill comes healing and restoration.

The limits of your thoughts are boundaries you set up yourself.

Pain, sorrow, and misery are the fruits of passion, which is the flower.

October Fifth

Where a person trapped by passion sees only injustice, a good person, who has conquered passion, sees cause and effect and recognizes the presence of Supreme Justice. Such a person can never feel they have been treated unfairly because they no longer see injustice. They know no one can cheat or harm them, for they have stopped cheating and harming themselves. No matter how people act toward them, it cannot cause them pain because they understand that everything they experience, even abuse or persecution, is the result of their own past actions. They view everything as good, rejoice in all things, and love their enemies, seeing them as instruments that help them repay their moral debts to the Great Law.

Supreme Justice and Supreme Love are one and the same.

The history of a nation is built upon its actions.

October Sixth

Just as a body is built of cells and a house is built of bricks, a person's mind is built of thoughts. The different characters of people are made up of different combinations of thoughts. This shows the truth of the saying, "As a man thinks in his heart, so is he."

Personal traits are just fixed thought patterns—they become part of a person's character. These traits can only be changed through a long effort of will and self-discipline. Character is built the same way as a house or a tree—by constantly adding new material, and that material is thought. Just as a city is built brick by brick, a person's character is built thought by thought.

Every person is a builder of their own mind.

October Seventh

Pure thoughts, when chosen wisely and placed well, are like durable bricks that will never crumble. From them, a strong and beautiful mind can be built, one that provides comfort and protection. Thoughts of strength, confidence, and duty—along with inspiring thoughts of a free, unselfish life—are useful bricks with which a solid mind-temple can be raised. To build such a temple, you must break down and destroy old and unhelpful habits of thought.

"Build bigger and better mansions for your soul as the seasons pass."
Each person is the builder of their own self.
Working in harmony with the basic laws of the universe.

October Eighth

If a person is to build a strong, successful, and exemplary life—a life that can withstand the storms of adversity and temptation—it must be based on a few simple, unwavering moral principles.

Four of these principles are Justice, Honesty, Sincerity, and Kindness. These four truths are to life what the four walls are to a house. If a person ignores these and tries to find success and happiness through injustice, deceit, and selfishness, they are like a builder who thinks they can create a strong house without paying attention to the proper arrangement of the walls. In the end, they will only find disappointment and failure.

Build like a true craftsman.

It is a mistake to think that little things can be ignored while focusing on greater things.

October Ninth

A person who follows the four moral principles as the foundation of their life and does not stray from them in their thoughts, words, or actions builds their character on a solid foundation of integrity. Such a person will inevitably build a life that brings them honor and peace. They are creating a strong and beautiful Temple of Life where they can rest in peace and happiness.

Anyone who wants a secure and blessed life must follow these moral principles in every aspect of it.

When aspiration is combined with concentration, the result is meditation.

October Tenth

When someone truly desires to live a higher, purer, and more radiant life than one focused on worldly pleasures, they are practicing aspiration. When they focus their thoughts on finding that life, they are practicing meditation.

Without deep aspiration, there can be no meditation. Lethargy and indifference destroy meditation. The more intense a person's nature, the easier it is for them to meditate and the more successful they will be. A passionate nature can quickly climb to the heights of Truth in meditation once it is awakened.

Meditation is essential for spiritual success.

When a person seeks to know and realize the Truth, they focus on self-purification and good conduct.

October Eleventh

Concentration can help a person reach great heights of genius, but it cannot bring them to the spiritual heights of Truth. To do that, they must meditate.

Through concentration, a person can gain great power, like Caesar. Through meditation, they can gain divine wisdom and perfect peace, like Buddha.

The goal of concentration is power; the goal of meditation is wisdom. Through concentration, a person gains skill in the tasks of life—in science, art, trade, and so on. Through meditation, they gain skill in life itself—in right living, enlightenment, and wisdom.

Saints, sages, and spiritual teachers are the result of holy meditation.

Love Truth with such devotion that you are completely absorbed in it.

October Twelfth

At first, the time spent in meditation may be short—perhaps just half an hour in the early morning—but the knowledge gained during that brief time of focused thought is carried into practice throughout the day. Therefore, meditation affects a person's entire life. As they advance in meditation, they become stronger, holier, calmer, and wiser, and they are better equipped to handle whatever life brings their way.

The principle of meditation has two parts:

Purifying the heart by repeatedly thinking about pure things.

Gaining divine knowledge by putting that purity into practice.

Through practice, association, and habit, thoughts tend to repeat themselves.

October Thirteenth

By dwelling daily on pure thoughts, a person who meditates forms a habit of pure and enlightened thinking. This leads to pure actions and well-done tasks. With constant repetition of pure thoughts, they eventually become one with those thoughts and live a purified life, shown in their pure actions and a serene and wise life.

Most people live in a state of conflicting desires, emotions, and thoughts, which leads to restlessness, uncertainty, and sorrow. But as a person trains their mind in meditation, they slowly gain control over this inner conflict by focusing their thoughts on a central principle.

It's easy to confuse daydreaming with meditation.

Selfishness, the root of all evil and suffering, grows from the dark soil of ignorance.

October Fourteenth

Both the rich and the poor suffer because of their selfishness, and no one is exempt. The rich have their sufferings, just as the poor do. Moreover, the rich often lose their riches, and the poor often acquire them. The poor person today may be the rich person tomorrow, and vice versa. Fear follows people like a shadow. The person who gains and holds wealth through selfish force will always feel insecure and afraid of losing it. Meanwhile, the poor person, who selfishly seeks or envies material wealth, will be tormented by the fear of poverty. And all people who live in this world of strife are overshadowed by one great fear—the fear of death.

Each person suffers because of their own selfishness.

The spirit is renewed and strengthened by meditating on spiritual things.

October fifteenth

A person must pass through three stages of letting go. The first is letting go of desire. The second is letting go of opinions. The third is letting go of the self. When someone begins to meditate, they will start to examine their desires, follow their effects in life, and see how they shape their character. They will quickly realize that without giving up desire, a person remains a prisoner of their own mind and their surroundings. Once this realization is made, they pass through the first gateway: the Surrender of Desire. Going through this gateway, they begin self-discipline, the first step toward purifying the soul.

The flame of faith must always be kept alive and carefully tended.

What we lose today will add to tomorrow's gain if our mind is focused on self-mastery.

October Sixteenth

Let a person press forward courageously, ignoring both the criticism from friends and the inner struggles with their own weaknesses. Aspire, search, and strive, always keeping their ideal in sight with eyes full of love. Each day, cleanse the mind of selfish motives and the heart of impure desires. Though they may stumble or fall, they continue onward and rise higher. At the end of each day, they should reflect in silence on their journey, without despairing, even if every day is marked by failures and falls. What matters is that some inner battle was fought, even if it wasn't won, and some silent victory was attempted, even if not achieved.

Learn to tell the difference between what is real and what is not, between the shadow and the substance.

Cultivate the priceless gift of spiritual discernment.

October Seventeenth

By clothing his soul in humility, a person puts all their effort into uprooting the opinions they once cherished. They begin to see the difference between the unchanging Truth and their own or others' changing opinions about it. They realize that their beliefs about Goodness, Purity, Compassion, and Love are not the same as these virtues themselves, and they must stand on these divine principles, not their own opinions. They once held their opinions in high regard, but now they no longer defend them against others and instead see them as worthless.

Stand on the divine principles of Purity, Wisdom, Compassion, and Love.

Find the divine center within yourself.

October Eighteenth

A person who is determined not to settle for appearances, shadows, or illusions will, by the strength of that resolve, see through every false image and discover the real substance of life. They will learn how to live and truly live. They will not be a slave to any passion, a servant to any opinion, or a follower of any mistaken belief. Finding the divine center within their heart, they will become pure, calm, strong, and wise, and constantly radiate the heavenly life they live—which is who they truly are.

To not know that changeless part of yourself, which defies time and death, is to not know anything and to play with fleeting reflections in the Mirror of Time.

Once a person takes refuge in the divine within themselves, they become free from sin. No doubt will shake their faith, no uncertainty will disturb their peace.

October Nineteenth

People love their desires because fulfillment feels sweet, but in the end, it brings pain and emptiness. They love the arguments of the intellect because ego feels desirable, but it leads to humiliation and sorrow. When the soul has tasted the bitter fruit of ego and the emptiness of gratification, it is ready to receive divine wisdom and enter the divine life. Only through the death of self can a person rise again into the immortal life, standing radiant in the wisdom of the heart.

Where the self disappears, the garden of heavenly life is found.

Life is more than just movement; it is Music. It is more than rest; it is Peace. More than work; it is Duty. And more than labor; it is Love.

October Twentieth

Let the impure turn to Purity, and they will become pure. Let the weak seek Strength, and they will become strong. Let the ignorant strive for Knowledge, and they will become wise. Everything is available to us, and we choose what we will have. Today, we choose in ignorance; tomorrow, we will choose in wisdom. We will work out our own salvation, whether we believe it or not, for we cannot escape ourselves or shift the eternal responsibility of our soul to another. No clever excuse or theological trick can deceive the Law of our being, which will shatter every selfish attempt to avoid right thinking and right action. Not even God can do for us what our soul is destined to achieve on its own.

Life is more than enjoyment; it is Blessedness.
To find Blessedness, one must find themselves.

October Twenty-first

People jump from belief to belief and find no rest. They travel to different lands, only to find disappointment. They build beautiful homes and plant pleasant gardens, yet find only boredom and discomfort. True rest and satisfaction are only found when a person looks within. When they build the inward Mansion of Faultless

Conduct, they discover endless and incorruptible joy. Once they have that, they infuse it into everything they do and own.

When a person can no longer bear the burden of their sins, they should turn to the Christ within their own heart, and they will find light-heartedness and join the glad company of the Immortals.

The spiritual heart of a person is the heart of the universe.

October Twenty-second

When someone dwells on the past or the future, they miss the present. They forget to live now. All things are possible now, and only now. Without wisdom, a person mistakes the unreal for the real and says, "If only I had done this last week, last month, or last year, things would be better today." Or they say, "I know what's best, and I'll do it tomorrow." Selfish people don't understand the immense value of the present and fail to see it as the only true reality, while the past and future are mere reflections. In truth, past and future don't exist except as shadows. Living in them—regretfully or selfishly—is to miss the real substance of life.

Let go of regret, stop dreaming of the future, and act now. That is wisdom.

October Twenty-third

Stop walking down the paths of dependence and wandering through the shadows of the past and future. Step into the open road and use your inner strength now. Whatever you want to be, you can be now. Failure comes from constantly postponing action, but the power to delay is also the power to act and achieve—constantly. Realize this truth, and you can become today the ideal person you dream of being.

Act now, and everything will be done. Live now, and you will find yourself in abundance. Be now, and you will realize you are already perfect.

Holiness comes from leaving sin unnoticed and letting it die along the way.

October Twenty-fourth

Tomorrow is always too late for anything. Whoever looks for help or salvation in tomorrow will fail and fall today. Did you fall yesterday? Did you sin greatly? Once you realize it, leave it behind instantly and forever. Focus on not sinning now. While you are mourning the past, your soul is unguarded against the sins of the present.

The foolish person loves the comfort of procrastination more than the firm path of present effort. They say, "I'll wake up early tomorrow. I'll get out of debt tomorrow. I'll do what I planned tomorrow." But the wise person knows the importance of the Eternal Now and wakes up early today, stays out of debt today, and acts on their intentions today. By doing so, they never stray from strength, peace, and fulfillment.

You won't rise by grieving over the unchangeable past but by fixing the present.

October Twenty-fifth

It is wise to leave behind what hasn't arrived and focus on what is here now, giving it your full attention and effort, leaving no room for regret.

A person's understanding is clouded by illusions of self. They think, "I was born on this day so many years ago, and I'll die at my appointed time." But in truth, they were never born, nor will they die, for how can something immortal be subject to birth and death? Once a person shakes off these illusions, they will see that the birth and death of the body are simply events in a journey, not the start or end of it.

The universe, with all it contains, is here and now.

If a person lets go of ego, they will see the universe in all its pure simplicity.

October Twenty-sixth

Life should no longer be lived in fragments but as a perfect whole. Only then will the simplicity of perfection be revealed. How can a fragment understand the whole? Yet it is simple for the whole to understand the fragment. How can sin perceive Holiness? Yet it is clear that Holiness understands sin. Whoever seeks to become greater must let go of the lesser. No form contains the circle, but the circle contains all forms. No color holds the light, but the light holds all colors. When a person destroys the forms of the self, they will see the Circle of Perfection.

When a person forgets (or annihilates) their personal self, they become a mirror reflecting the universal Reality without flaw.

Just as the single note is part of the perfect chord, the drop of water is useful only by losing itself in the ocean.

October Twenty-seventh

Sink yourself with compassion into the heart of humanity, and you will reflect the harmonies of Heaven. Lose yourself in unlimited love for all, and you will create lasting works and become one with the eternal Ocean of Bliss.

Human beings first evolve outward into complexity, then turn back to central simplicity. When someone realizes they cannot understand the universe without knowing themselves, they begin the journey toward Original Simplicity. They start to grow from within, and as they grow, they embrace the universe.

Stop speculating about God and discover the all-encompassing Good within you.

The pure person knows themselves as pure being.

October Twenty-eighth

Whoever refuses to give up their secret desires, greed, anger, or opinions can neither see nor know anything. They will remain ignorant in the school of Wisdom, even if others see them as learned.

To find the key to Knowledge, a person must first find themselves. Your sins are not part of who you are; they are like diseases you have come to love. Let go of them, and they will let go of you. When they fall away, your true self will be revealed. You will know yourself as Clear Vision, Invincible Principle, Immortal Life, and Eternal Good.

Purity is simple and needs no argument to support it.

Truth lives itself.

October Twenty-ninth

Meekness, Patience, Love, Compassion, and Wisdom—these are the qualities of Original Simplicity. Therefore, those who are imperfect cannot understand it. Only wisdom can understand wisdom, so the foolish person says, "No one is wise." The imperfect person says, "No one can be perfect," and thus remains as they are. Even if they live with a perfect person all their life, they won't see their perfection. They will mistake Meekness for cowardice, Patience and Compassion for weakness, and Wisdom for foolishness. True discernment belongs to the Perfect Whole, not to any part. So people are advised not to judge until they have manifested the Perfect Life.

A life without fault is the only true witness to Truth.

Whoever has found the reality within themselves has found the original and universal Reality.

October Thirtieth

By knowing the divine heart within, all hearts are known. The thoughts of all people become known to someone who has mastered their own thoughts. That's why a good person does not defend themselves but molds others to their own likeness.

Just as the transcendent solves the basic, so Pure Goodness solves all problems. All problems disappear when Pure Goodness is achieved, which is why a good person is called "The Slayer of Illusions." What problem can remain where sin does not exist?

To those who strive tirelessly without rest, retreat into the quiet holiness of your own being and live from there. In doing so, you will find Pure Goodness, tear apart the Veil of Illusion, and enter into the Peace, Patience, and Glory of Perfection, for Pure Goodness and Original Simplicity are one.

So simple is Original Simplicity that a person must let go of everything to see it.

Those who seek approval from others will experience great pain and unrest.

October Thirty-first

To detach from every outward thing and rely solely on inner virtue is Unfailing Wisdom. A person with this wisdom remains unchanged whether in riches or poverty. Riches cannot add to their strength, nor can poverty take away their serenity.

A wise person refuses to be enslaved by outward things or events and instead sees everything as useful for learning and growth. They view all events as good and, with no focus on evil, they grow wiser every day. They make use of everything, placing everything under their control. They recognize their mistakes as soon as they happen and accept them as valuable lessons, knowing there are no mistakes in the Divine Order.

To love where love is not returned—that is a strength that will never fail.

The wise person is eager to learn but never anxious to teach.

November First.

All strength, wisdom, power, and knowledge can be found within, but they will not be found in selfishness. They are only discovered in obedience, humility, and a willingness to learn. One must follow higher principles and not indulge in lower impulses. If a person stands on ego, rejecting correction and guidance, they are bound to fall; in fact, they have already fallen. A great teacher once said to his followers, "Those who rely only on themselves, using truth as their guide, and not depending on outside help, will reach the highest heights! But they must be willing to learn." The true teacher lives in every person's heart.

Scattering your thoughts leads to weakness; focusing them leads to power.

November Second

Things are useful, and thoughts are powerful when they are concentrated. Purpose is concentrated thought. All mental energy is aimed at reaching a goal, and obstacles in the way are overcome one by one. Purpose is the cornerstone of success. It holds together what would otherwise be scattered and ineffective. Empty whims, fleeting fancies, vague desires, and half-hearted efforts have no place in purpose. When there is a firm decision to accomplish something, it carries an unstoppable force that sweeps away all lesser distractions and leads to victory.

All successful people are driven by purpose.

Know this: you make and unmake yourself.

November Third

Doubt, worry, and anxiety are like shadows that exist only in the lower self and will no longer trouble the person who rises to the higher, peaceful state of their soul. Grief, too, will disappear for anyone who understands the Law of their being. When someone truly understands this Law, they will find that it is Love, an eternal and unbreakable Love. They will become one with Love, and by loving all, with a mind free of hatred and foolishness, they will receive the invincible protection that Love offers. Not asking for anything, they will lose nothing. Not seeking pleasure, they will find no sorrow. Using all their abilities for service, they will live in the highest state of peace and joy.

You are a slave if you choose to be; you are a master if you choose to make yourself one.

He who finds meekness has found divinity.

November Fourth

The mountain doesn't bow to the strongest storm, but it protects the bird and the lamb. Even though everyone walks on it, it supports them, holding them up with its unshakeable strength. In the same way, the meek person is unmoved by anything but still bends down to help the smallest creature. Though they may be despised, they lift everyone up and protect them with love.

Just as the mountain stands tall and majestic in silent strength, so does the divine person stand in silent meekness. Their compassion, like the mountain's strength, is boundless and sublime. While their body may be grounded in the valleys and mists, their soul reaches the highest peaks, forever bathed in unclouded light, living in harmony with the Silence.

The meek person has realized their divine nature and knows themselves as divine.

The meek person lives without fear, knowing the Highest, and having the lowest beneath their feet.

November Fifth

The meek person shines even in darkness and flourishes in the quiet. Meekness doesn't boast, doesn't advertise itself, and doesn't thrive on attention. It is practiced, seen, and unseen, and because it's a spiritual quality, it's only noticed by the spiritual eye. Those who aren't spiritually awake can't see it or appreciate it, being drawn to worldly displays and appearances. History doesn't record the actions of the meek, as its glory is in conflict and self-importance. The meek person's glory lies in peace and gentleness, which the world doesn't recognize but silently honors long after the meek have withdrawn.

The meek person is revealed during times of trial; when others fall, they stand.

The meek person resists nothing, and in doing so, conquers everything.

November Sixth

Anyone who thinks they can be harmed by others and seeks to defend themselves doesn't understand meekness or the true meaning of life.

"He insulted me, he beat me, he wronged me, he took from me." Those who hold onto such thoughts will never escape hatred, for hatred only ends by love. What does it matter if someone speaks falsely about you? A lie is a lie, and that's the end of it. It has no power to hurt you unless you choose to be hurt by it. What matters more is that you try to defend yourself, for by doing so, you give life to the lie, allowing it to harm you.

Remove all evil from your own heart, and you will see the foolishness of resisting it in others.

November Seventh

Purpose goes hand in hand with intelligence. There are small purposes and great purposes, depending on the level of intelligence. A great mind will always have a great purpose. A weak intelligence will lack purpose. A wandering mind shows a lack of development.

The people who have shaped human history were people of strong purpose. Like a Roman building a road, they followed a clear path and refused to turn aside, even when faced with torture or death. The Great Leaders of humanity are the mental path-makers, and the rest of us follow the intellectual and spiritual roads they've paved.

Inert matter yields to a living force, and circumstances yield to the power of purpose.

In the end, everything gives way to the silent, unstoppable energy of purpose.

November Eighth

The weak person who feels miserable because they're misunderstood won't achieve much. The vain person who compromises their goals to please others won't achieve greatness. The double-minded person who tries to compromise their purpose will fail. The person of unwavering purpose, who stands firm in the face of misunderstandings, false accusations, flattery, or empty promises, is the one who will achieve excellence, success, greatness, and power.

Challenges inspire the person with purpose. Difficulties drive them to try harder. Mistakes, losses, and pain don't bring them down, and failures are steps to success because they're always aware of their ultimate victory.

The strength of purpose grows stronger as obstacles grow bigger.

Joy always accompanies a task that is successfully completed.

November Ninth

Of all unhappy people, the person who avoids work is the most miserable. Thinking that avoiding difficult tasks will bring peace, they instead find their mind is always restless. They feel ashamed inside and lose their sense of honor and self-respect. "He who refuses to work according to his abilities will perish by his own needs," said Carlyle. It's a moral law that a person who avoids their duties and doesn't work to the best of their abilities begins to fade away—first in their character, then in their body and circumstances. Life and action are the same thing, and when someone tries to avoid effort, either mental or physical, they begin to decay.

A completed task always brings peace and satisfaction.

The price of life is effort.

November Tenth

Every successful achievement, even in worldly matters, is rewarded with a certain amount of joy. In spiritual matters, the joy that follows the fulfillment of purpose is deep and lasting. There's a unique joy, though hard to describe, when, after many failed attempts, a deeply rooted character flaw is finally overcome, never to trouble the person or the world again. Those striving for virtue, working to build a noble character, feel joy with every step they take in mastering themselves. This joy never leaves but becomes a permanent part of their spiritual nature.

The reward for success is joy.

November Eleventh

As you think, you move forward. As you love, you attract. Where you are today is a result of your past thoughts, and where you'll be tomorrow depends on your thoughts today. You can't escape the results of your thinking, but you can endure them and learn, accept them, and be glad.

You will always arrive at the place where your deepest love, your strongest thoughts, lead you. If your love is lowly, you'll end up in a lowly place. If it's beautiful, you'll reach a beautiful place.

You can change your thoughts and, by doing so, change your life. You are powerful, not powerless.

Nothing is predetermined; everything is shaped.

The person who thinks, speaks, and acts sincerely is surrounded by sincere friends. The insincere person is surrounded by insincere friends.

November Twelfth

Every fact and process in nature contains a moral lesson for the wise. There is no law in the world that doesn't operate with the same certainty in the mind and life of humans. All of Jesus' parables demonstrate this truth and are drawn from simple facts in nature. There is a process of planting seeds in the mind and life, just as in a field, and the kind of seeds planted determines the kind of harvest. Thoughts, words, and actions are seeds, and by the unbreakable law of life, they produce after their kind.

The person who thinks hateful thoughts attracts hatred. The person who thinks loving thoughts is loved.

When you understand yourself, you'll see that every event in your life is weighed in perfect fairness.

The person who wants to be blessed must spread blessings.

November Thirteenth

The farmer scatters all his seeds on the land and then leaves them to the elements. If he selfishly hoarded his seeds, he would lose both the seeds and the harvest because the seeds would rot. They die when he plants them, but in dying, they bring a greater abundance. It's the same in life: we get by giving, and we grow rich by sharing.

The person who claims they have knowledge but won't share it because the world isn't ready either doesn't have that knowledge or will soon lose it. To hoard is to lose; to hold on too tightly is to be emptied.

The person who wants to be happy must consider the happiness of others.

People reap what they sow.

November Fourteenth

If someone is troubled, confused, sad, or unhappy, they should ask themselves:

"What mental seeds have I been planting?"
"What seeds am I planting now?"
"What is my attitude toward others?"

"What seeds of trouble and sadness have I sown that I am now harvesting these bitter fruits?"

They should search within, find the answers, and once they've found them, abandon all selfish seeds and start planting only seeds of Truth. They should learn from the farmer the simple truths of wisdom and scatter seeds of kindness, gentleness, and love.

The way to find peace and joy is to scatter peaceful and joyful thoughts, words, and actions.

By destroying the idols of self, we move closer to the great, quiet Heart of Love.

November Fifteenth.

December First.

Contentment is a virtue that becomes high and spiritual as the mind learns to understand and the heart opens to the guidance of a merciful law.

Being content doesn't mean giving up effort; it means freeing effort from anxiety. It doesn't mean being satisfied with sin, ignorance, or foolishness, but rather resting happily in the completion of duty and work.

A person might seem content with living poorly, staying in sin or debt, but their true state is indifference to their duty, obligations, and what they owe others. Such a person doesn't really have the virtue of contentment, nor do they experience the pure and lasting joy that comes with active achievement.

True contentment comes from honest effort and living rightly.

The truly content person works hard and faithfully and accepts all results with a peaceful heart.

December Second

There are three things a person should be content with: whatever happens, their friendships and possessions, and their pure thoughts. Being content with whatever happens will keep them from grief. Being content with their friendships and possessions will keep them free from anxiety and misery. Being content with their pure thoughts will keep them from falling back into impurities.

There are three things a person should not be content with: their opinions, their character, and their spiritual condition. By not being content with their opinions, they will keep growing in intelligence. By not being content with their character, they will keep growing in strength and virtue. By not being content with their spiritual condition, they will enter into greater wisdom and blessedness every day.

Results match effort.

Universal Brotherhood is the ultimate ideal for humanity, and the world is slowly but surely moving toward that ideal.

December Third

Brotherhood, as an organization among humans, cannot exist as long as selfishness rules the hearts of those who join together for any cause. Selfishness will eventually tear apart any attempt at loving unity.

But although organized brotherhood has largely failed, any person can realize brotherhood in its perfect form and understand its beauty if they make themselves wise, pure, and loving. By removing every element of conflict from their mind and practicing divine qualities, they will experience true brotherhood.

Wherever discord exists in a heart, brotherhood is not realized.

Brotherhood begins as a spiritual state, and its outer expression in the world follows naturally.

December Fourth

From the spirit of humility come gentleness and peace. From self-surrender come patience, wisdom, and true judgment. From love come kindness, joy, and harmony. And from compassion come gentleness and forgiveness.

A person who aligns themselves with these four qualities becomes divinely enlightened. They understand why people act as they do and where those actions lead, so they no longer live in dark tendencies like envy, bitterness, or judgment. They have realized brotherhood in its fullest form, free from malice and strife.

Everyone, whether living in darkness or light, is their brother. They have only goodwill toward all.

Where there is pride, self-love, hatred, or judgment, brotherhood cannot exist.

Brotherhood starts with abandoning selfishness.

December Fifth

There are many theories and plans for promoting brotherhood, but true brotherhood itself is unchanging. It's found only in giving up selfishness and conflict while practicing goodwill and peace. Brotherhood is something to be practiced, not theorized about. Self-surrender and goodwill protect it, and peace is where it resides.

When two people are determined to hold onto opposing opinions, selfishness and ill-will are present, and brotherhood is absent.

When two people are ready to sympathize with each other, to see no evil in each other, and to serve instead of attack each other, brotherhood is present.

Brotherhood is only practiced and understood by those whose hearts are at peace with the world.

Prejudice and cruelty are inseparable.

December Sixth

Sympathy is not needed for those who are purer and wiser than oneself. Instead, one should show respect and strive to reach their level. No one can fully understand someone wiser than themselves, and before criticizing them, one should ask if they are truly better than the person they are judging. If they are better, let them offer sympathy. If not, let them offer respect.

When someone is quick to judge and condemn others, they should first reflect on their own shortcomings.

Dislike, resentment, and condemnation are all forms of hatred, and evil will not end until these feelings are removed from the heart.

December Seventh

Forgetting injuries done to us is only the beginning of wisdom. There is a better way—one where the heart and mind are so purified that there are no injuries to remember. Only pride and selfishness can be hurt by others' actions and words. When these are removed from the heart, one will no longer feel injured or wronged by others.

A pure heart leads to a true understanding of things. And from that understanding comes a life of peace, free from bitterness and suffering.

Those troubled by the sins of others are far from the truth.

Those troubled by their own sins are very near the gate of wisdom.

December Eighth

The person who holds onto resentment cannot know peace or understand the truth. But the person who banishes resentment will find peace and understanding.

The person who has removed evil from their own heart cannot resent it in others, because they understand its true nature and origin. They see it as a mistake made out of ignorance. With greater understanding, sin becomes impossible. Those who sin don't understand; those who understand don't sin.

A pure person keeps their heart tender toward those who wrongly believe they can harm them. They are not troubled by others' wrong attitudes toward them. Their heart rests in compassion and love.

Those who aim to live rightly must calmly and wisely seek understanding.

A pure heart and a righteous life are of the utmost importance.

December Ninth

Actions and thoughts that cause suffering come from self-interest and selfishness. Thoughts and actions that bring happiness come from truth.

The process of transforming the mind is twofold: meditation and practice. Through meditation, one finds the foundation for right actions, and through practice, one carries out those actions in daily life.

Truth is not learned from books, arguments, or debates. It's learned through right actions.

Truth is only gained through practice.

December Tenth

Anyone who wants to gain truth must practice it. They must begin with self-control, master it, and then move on to the next lesson until they achieve moral perfection. Many people believe that truth lies in holding certain ideas or opinions. They read books, form an opinion, call it truth, and then argue with others to prove their opinion is correct.

In worldly matters, people are wise enough to act in order to reach their goals, but in spiritual matters, they often just read without taking action and believe they have found truth.

True truth is shown through a pure and blameless life.

Love is all-encompassing.

December Eleventh

Love cannot belong exclusively to any religion, sect, or group. Any claim that one particular doctrine holds exclusive truth is a denial of love.

Truth is a spirit and a way of life. While it can be expressed through many doctrines, it can never be confined to one.

Love is like an angel with wings. It can't be tied down to any doctrine. It is bigger than all opinions, philosophies, or beliefs. Love includes everyone—the good and the bad, the clean and the unclean.

The person whose love is wide enough to include all people has the most religion, wisdom, and understanding because they see people as they truly are.

Hatred is the absence of love and, therefore, the absence of all that comes with love.

Love expands a person's mind until it embraces all humanity.

December Twelfth

The way of love is the way of life—eternal life. The first step on this path is getting rid of criticism, quarrels, fault-finding, and suspicion.

If these habits control us, we do not have love.

To be honest with ourselves is the first step toward finding love. But to deceive ourselves keeps us from it.

If we want to grow in love, we must start by removing mean and suspicious thoughts about others. We must learn to treat people with generosity and try to understand their reasons for their actions, even when they seem to go against our own. When we do this, we will eventually love them with the deep love that St. Paul describes—a love that is a lasting principle.

Whoever has love, no matter their religion, is enlightened by the light of truth.

The life of truth is one where wrong thoughts and actions are left behind and right thoughts and actions are embraced.

December Thirteenth

It is the wrong actions of people that bring unhappiness into the world. It will be right actions that turn misery into joy.

By doing wrong, we find sorrow. By doing right, we find happiness.

But a person must not think, "It's the wrong actions of others that make me unhappy." This thought breeds bitterness and hatred. They must realize that their unhappiness comes from something wrong within themselves. It's a sign that they are still imperfect and have something within that needs to be strengthened.

They must never blame others for their own missteps or troubles but instead work on becoming more steadfast in heart and firmly rooted in the truth.

Walk humbly along the path of truth.

The principles of truth are unchanging and cannot be altered by anyone.

December Fourteenth

The principles of truth were discovered through searching and practice, and they have been shared to make the path clearer for others.

This is the path that all beings travel when moving from sin to sinlessness, from error to truth.

It is the ancient path walked by every saint, Buddha, and Christ on their way to divine perfection. And it's the same path every imperfect person will take in the future to reach that glorious goal.

It doesn't matter what religion someone follows. If they are daily working on overcoming their own sins and purifying their heart, they are walking this path.

Religions change with time, but the principles of divine virtue remain the same forever.

Truth is one, though it can be seen in many ways and is adaptable to people in different stages of growth.

December Fifteenth.

We have learned from all the Great Teachers, and our joy has been immense in finding the same divine qualities and truths in the lives and teachings of the gentle Indian and Chinese Teachers as in Jesus Christ. We see them all as wonderful, admirable, and so great, good, and wise that we can only show them reverence and learn from them. They have had a profound positive influence on the different people they taught and have earned the undying respect and worship of millions.

Great Teachers are like the finest flowers of humanity, showing what all men can become one day.

Perfect purity of heart frees a person from all selfish desires and cravings.

December Sixteenth

There is a clear difference between a worldly life and a religious life. A person who follows their impure desires every day without wanting to give them up is irreligious. But the one who works every day to control and eliminate those impure desires is truly religious.

A religious person should control their passions and desires because that's what religion is. They need to see people and things as they are and understand that everyone is living according to their nature, choosing their own paths as intelligent beings. They must never push their rules onto others or think of themselves as being on a "higher level" than others. They should put themselves in other people's shoes and see things from their perspective.

A lover of truth must also love all people and let that love flow without limits.

The moral law is like a mathematical truth that gives us certainty and security in life.

December Seventeenth

Life's constant changes, uncertainties, and mysteries make it necessary to find a solid foundation to maintain happiness and peace of mind. This foundation is best described as Divine Justice. Human justice varies depending on each person's understanding, but Divine Justice never changes and keeps the universe balanced. Divine Justice is like spiritual mathematics, where, just like numbers, two and two always make four.

When the same cause happens, the same effect will always follow.

All spiritual laws are as infallible as the laws of the physical world.

December Eighteenth

When a person acts in the same way under the same circumstances, the result will always be the same. Without this basic ethical justice, society could not survive because it is the fair reactions to people's actions that keep society from falling apart.

The differences in happiness and suffering in life come from moral forces working with perfect accuracy. This flawless accuracy is the fundamental certainty in life. Finding this law helps a person become perfect, wise, and filled with peace and joy.

The moral order of the universe must be balanced, or else everything would collapse.

Nothing is higher than doing what is right.

December Nineteenth

If a person loses belief in this basic certainty, they are lost in a sea of chance without any direction. They have no foundation for building their character or life, no motivation for good deeds, and no center for moral action. They have no place of peace or safety.

Even the simplest idea of God as a perfect being who doesn't make mistakes reflects belief in this principle of Divine Justice.

According to this principle, there is no favoritism or chance—only unchanging right. All human suffering is the result of mistakes caused by ignorance, but these effects will eventually pass away.

No one can suffer for something they didn't do or fail to do because that would be an effect without a cause.

December Twentieth

Talent, genius, goodness, and greatness are not just given to the world already complete. They are the result of a long chain of causes and effects.

We can see the process of growth in a flower, but although we don't always see mental growth in the same way, it is still happening.

I said that mental growth is not visible, but this is only partly true. The wise person sees spiritual growth with their inner eye. Just like a scientist understands natural causes and effects, the wise person understands spiritual causes and effects. They see how characters, like plants, grow over time. When they see the flowers of genius and virtue bloom, they know the seeds that started them and how they grew over long periods of silent development.

Nothing appears fully formed. There is always a process of change and growth.

Awakening to this vision calls us to live a higher life.

December Twenty-first

Just as a person cannot live in two countries at the same time, they cannot live in two spiritual worlds at once. They must leave behind the world of sin before they can live in the world of truth.

When someone moves to a new country, they leave behind all their beloved associations, dear friends, and family. Everything they once loved must be left behind. In the same way, when someone chooses to live in the world of truth, they must give up the old world of error, including its pleasures, cherished sins, and false connections.

By letting go of these things, both the individual and humanity as a whole benefit, making the universe a brighter place.

We must shake off the mud from the valley to experience the peace of the mountain.

Right thoughts come from the right mental attitude and lead to right actions.

December Twenty-second

The right mental attitude looks for the good in every life experience and draws strength, knowledge, and wisdom from it.

Right thoughts are full of cheer, joy, hope, confidence, courage, constant love, generosity, and strong faith. These positive affirmations build strong characters, useful lives, and the kind of personal successes that advance the world. These thoughts naturally lead to right actions—putting forth energy and effort into work and achieving legitimate goals. Just like a climber reaches the top of a mountain, the hard-working, cheerful person eventually reaches their goal.

Throughout history, successful people have achieved their success by working for it.

Suffering is a purifying and perfecting process.

December Twenty-third

Causing others to suffer only leads to deeper ignorance. But when we suffer ourselves, we grow closer to enlightenment. Pain teaches us to be kind and compassionate. It softens our hearts and makes us more thoughtful of others' pain.

When someone does something cruel, they think that's the end of it. But in reality, it's only the beginning. That action brings a series of consequences that lead to their suffering.

For every wrong thought or unkind action, we must face some form of mental or physical pain, and the kind of pain will match the initial thought or action.

Suffering teaches us to understand and feel for the suffering of others.

Every resource you need is already within you.

December Twenty-fourth

Just like doing small tasks with strength leads to greater strength, doing them weakly leads to more weakness. A person's character is made up of all the little things they do.

Weakness is as much a source of suffering as sin, and true happiness can't be found until a person develops strength of character.

The weak person grows strong by valuing little things and doing them with care. The strong person becomes weak by neglecting small things, losing their wisdom, and wasting their energy.

The only way to grow in strength and wisdom is by acting wisely and strongly in the present moment.

The year is passing, and it's a blessing to let go of its mistakes and wrongs forever, never to remember them again.

December Twenty-fifth

The past is gone and cannot be changed, so let it fade away. But hold on to its lessons and use them to strengthen yourself now. Let those lessons be the starting points for a better, purer, more perfect life in the coming years.

Let all thoughts of hatred, resentment, and strife die with the passing year. Wipe away from your heart all bad memories and grudges.

Let the message of "Peace on earth and goodwill to men," which is repeated by many during this season, be more than just words to you. Let it become your way of life, living in your heart without being disturbed by thoughts of ill-will.

Blessed is the person who has no wrongs to remember and no injuries to forgive, whose heart is too pure to hold hateful thoughts about others.

December Twenty-sixth

Don't see your difficulties as signs of bad things to come. If you do, you'll make them bad. Instead, see them as signs of good, because that's what they truly are.

Don't fool yourself into thinking you can escape them—you can't. Don't try to run from them either, because wherever you go, they will follow.

Face them calmly and bravely. Analyze their strength, understand them, and then conquer them.

By doing this, you will develop strength and intelligence. You will find paths to happiness that others cannot see.

There is no peace in sin, no rest in error. True peace is only found in wisdom.

Go to your tasks with love in your heart, and you will go to them with joy and lightness.

December Twenty-seventh

What heavy burden does a person carry that isn't made heavier by weak thoughts or selfish desires?

If your situation is "difficult," it's because you need it, and you can develop the strength to handle it.

It's difficult because there's a weakness in you, and it will continue to be difficult until you fix that weakness.

Be grateful for the chance to grow stronger and wiser. Wisdom doesn't find circumstances difficult, and love doesn't get tired.

Stop dwelling on your own difficult situations and think about the lives of others around you.

The duty you avoid is like an angel correcting you, and the pleasure you chase after is like a flattering enemy.

December Twenty-eighth

There are small selfish indulgences that may seem harmless, but no selfish indulgence is without harm.

People don't realize what they lose by giving in to selfish gratifications, even when they seem innocent or sweet.

If the divine nature within us is to rise strong and victorious, the animal nature within us must die.

Every time you give in to selfish cravings, even when they seem harmless, you make them stronger and give them more control over your mind, which should belong to the truth.

Live above the craving for excitement and you will live a life that is neither empty nor uncertain.

Sacrifice hatred and offer it up as a sign of devotion to others.

December Twenty-ninth

Whatever people may say or do to you, never take offense. Don't respond to hate with more hate.

If someone hates you, maybe you've made a mistake, either knowingly or unknowingly. Or maybe it's just a misunderstanding that a little kindness and reason could fix.

But in any case, saying "Father, forgive them" is always better than "I will never deal with them again."

Hatred is small, blind, and miserable. Love is great, wise, and joyful.

Open your heart to let in that sweet, great, and beautiful love that includes everyone.

December Thirtieth

Selfishness leads to misery, while unselfishness leads to joy—not just for yourself, but for everyone around you.

Because all of humanity is connected, the joy of one person is the joy of everyone.

Knowing this, let us spread kindness and not thorns along life's path. Even in the paths of our enemies, let us spread the blossoms of unselfish love.

So as they walk along, their footprints will fill the air with the fragrance of holiness, making the world a happier place.

Seek the highest good, and you will taste the deepest joy.

December Thirty-first

The universe doesn't play favorites. It is completely just, and each person receives exactly what they earn.

Happy is the person who has found that life where selfish thoughts are gone.

Even now, in this life, they have entered the Kingdom of Heaven and rest in the arms of the Infinite.

Sweet is the peace and deep the joy of the person who has freed their heart from lust, hatred, and dark desires.

The one who can sincerely bless all living things, without any bitterness or selfishness, has found the fullness of peace and Perfect Blessedness.

Man can find the right path in life, and once found, can rejoice and be glad.

Thank you for Reading

You've Just Read a Piece of the Greatest Library Ever Rebuilt

Thank you for reading.

This book is one of thousands we're restoring, reimagining, and translating as part of the **Modern Library of Alexandria** — a global movement to preserve and share humanity's most important ideas.

What was once lost to fire and time is now rising again — not just as memory, but as living, breathing knowledge, freely accessible to all.

What You Can Do Next:

- **Keep Reading.**

  Discover more legendary works — in beautiful print, audiobook, or digital form — at LibraryofAlexandria.com.

- **Build Your Own Library.**

  Every title is available as a paperback, hardcover, or collectible boxset — at true printing cost. Craft a personal library worthy of display.

- **Spread the Light.**

  Share this book. Tell others about the movement. Help us translate every timeless work into every language, so no reader is ever left behind.

By finishing this book, you've already taken part in something extraordinary.

Join us at LibraryofAlexandria.com

Together, we're rebuilding the greatest library the world has ever known.

With appreciation,
The Modern Library of Alexandria Team

Visit:

www.libraryofalexandria.com

Or scan the code below: